Understanding Education Research

UNDERSTANDING EDUCATION RESEARCH

A Guide to Critical Reading

Gary Shank
Launcelot Brown
Janice Pringle

Routledge
Taylor & Francis Group

LONDON AND NEW YORK

First published 2014 by Paradigm Publishers

Published 2016 by Routledge
2 Park Square, Milton Park, Abingdon, Oxon OX14 4RN
711 Third Avenue, New York, NY 10017, USA

Routledge is an imprint of the Taylor & Francis Group, an informa business

Copyright © 2014 , Taylor & Francis.

Library of Congress Cataloging-in-Publication Data

Shank, Gary D.
  Understanding education research : a guide to critical reading / Gary Shank, Launcelot Brown, Janice Pringle.
    pages cm
  Includes bibliographical references and index.
  ISBN 978-1-61205-581-7 (pbk.   )
  ISBN 978-1-61205-639-5 (consumer e-book)
  1. Education—Research—Methodology. I. Brown, Launcelot. II. Pringle, Janice. III. Title.
  LB1028.S4395 2014
  370.72—dc23

                                        2013045264

Designed and Typeset in New Baskerville by Straight Creek Bookmakers.

ISBN 13: 978-1-61205-581-7 (pbk)
ISBN 13: 978-1-61205-580-0 (hbk)

Contents

Preface

The Role of Research

This book is not only about the role of research in the field of education. More than that, this book is about research not just as a tool for looking at how to understand and improve education, but as a process that is fundamental to education itself.

Before we talk about how fundamental research is to education, we first must talk about how fundamental education itself is. We have argued for some time that education is a basic human process (Shank, 2005). That is, education is as fundamental as any other basic human experience. We eat, we sleep, we seek companionship, we create and raise our young, we seek shelter, and we teach and learn from each other.

Try this little experiment. Look at any group of people gathered informally. Once they start talking to each other, within minutes they are teaching and learning. We see this in just about every human setting. It is part of our nature as human beings. Therefore, it should come as no surprise to us that education pervades every aspect of human culture.

Human beings specialize and institutionalize many of their basic processes. For instance, we don't just seek food. We also go to specialty supermarkets and Chinese restaurants, for example. Education is no different. We have created many formal systems of education. Our system of public education is the biggest example, and the one that professionally engages most of us.

When we look at schooling as a formal system, we see that it has many components. Professional researchers do their work because they want to improve the way things work, or sometimes just because they are curious and want answers to basic questions. That is, research on its own terms can be just as basic as any other aspect of education. We all are curious and we all want to make things better. But research goes further, in its service to teachers.

Teachers, for their part, need to be able to deliver accurate and up-to-date information to their students. They need to be able to organize that material so that it is quickly and easily learned. They need to be able to check and see what their students are learning and not learning. They need to be able to manage their students as individuals and as groups in order for them to sustain a proper climate for learning. The list goes on and on.

When we look at the areas discussed above, they all have at least one thing in common—they all depend on ongoing research efforts in order to realize their potential to students and teachers. That is, without research, there is no formal process of schooling, as we know it. If research stopped, teachers would soon be teaching out-of-date material. They would be dependent on learning and behavioral strategies that might not be able to address the needs of our ever-changing society. There would be at least stagnation, and at worst a disconnection between our culture and our educational process. For these, and for many other reasons that we have not mentioned, research is a fundamental part of the educational system.

As we move forward, we need to look at our relationship to research, and how this affects our roles as educational professionals.

Features of This Book

As you read on in this book you will find features and information that will

- Provide a step-by-step breakdown of the form and logic of research articles
- Develop critical reading skills
- Provide a practical sense of the skills being presented, through exercises throughout the book
- Offer a framework for questions helpful in critically engaging research materials, and ways to discover answers
- Explore the idea of research literacy as a necessary skill

As we move forward, we need to look at our relationship to research, and how this affects our roles as educational professionals. We begin this process in the next chapter.

Chapter One

Research Literacy and the Research Critic

As we have already argued, research is a fundamental part of the educational profession. No matter what you do in this field, from being a teacher or administrator to being a researcher yourself, you need to be able to address the flood of ongoing research that is constantly being produced. Another way to put this is to say that you need to be *research literate*.

What Is Research Literacy?

Once upon a time, there was only literacy, or what we might call basic literacy. Basic literacy involved the ability to read and write (see Adler & Van Doren, 1972; Bloom, 2001). People who cannot read or write are called *illiterate*. As you can imagine, it is quite a stigma in our culture to be illiterate. However, there have been times and cultures where no one, or only a handful of people, were literate. Those cultures were called *oral cultures*. People in oral cultures were not stupid or backward; they just lived in a culture where reading and writing were not the norm and therefore were not necessary for being able to function successfully in that culture (Ong, 1982).

Nowadays, there are almost no purely oral cultures left—at least in regards to basic literacy. Reading and writing are required skills at all levels of life for most of us. However, there are also other forms of literacy. Some of the more specialized forms of literacy involve things like math literacy and science literacy and art literacy and sports literacy and film literacy and cultural literacy and so on. All of these specialized "literacies" employ their own set of crucial concepts and quite often their own specialized languages. As a result, most of us are not all that "literate" in art or sports or film or cultural studies. We can appreciate these areas, but usually at a more basic consumer level. We leave it to the experts, or the critics, in those areas to guide us and help us select what is valuable and what is trivial for us.

At one time in the field of professional education, it was considered adequate to be able to follow the advice of researchers and not to have to worry about whether we could understand the nuts and bolts of their research ourselves. To put it another way, it was not necessary for us to be research literate. But that time has passed. We are now in an era where everyone in the field of education, from teachers to administrators to professors to researchers, needs to develop a complete and comprehensive picture of how research functions. We call this *research literacy*. In order to be research literate, the person needs to know

- The basic principles of qualitative and quantitative research in education
- How research articles are put together
- How to read research articles at increasingly more complex levels
- How to evaluate the quality of the research

When people are able to read and evaluate research articles at these very high levels, they are more than just research literate. They can rightfully be called *research critics*. One of the main goals of this book is to help put you on the road not just toward research literacy, but toward becoming a research critic yourself. To do this, we need to start with a clear understanding of what a research critic really is.

What Is a Research Critic?

If we think of the field of education as a community where people do different things, there are four basic roles that each and every one of us in the larger community might play. The best way to think of these roles is to imagine them as falling along a spectrum.

At the near end of the spectrum are those people in this culture who play no direct role in the educational community. They are no longer in school, nor do they have children who are being educated. We can call these people *invested bystanders*. Invested bystanders, however, are not neutral about education. Even though they (or their families) are not being educated per se, they are being affected by how good or how poor education as a process is being performed. Furthermore, and this is a major point, most of them are also helping to pay (via their taxes) for the education of all our children as a whole.

The better the education system in their communities, for instance, the lower the crime rate and the more likely some of these invested bystanders will be able to find skilled workers and service providers. So invested bystanders tend to care very much about the quality of education. That concern, however, is almost always in terms of results. That is, how well is education meeting their larger social and cultural needs? So while invested bystanders might refine their understanding of educational research and its findings to some degree, most often they are content to leave the details to others (so long as the educational system is producing its desired results).

At the complete other end of the spectrum are those people who are most active in the formulation, creation, and dissemination of actual educational research projects and findings. These people are the *researchers*. Researchers need to have the most direct and comprehensive and up-to-date knowledge and understanding of educational research as a whole. That is, they need to know what types of research have been conducted, past and present; how to do research; and how to communicate research findings to others. To become a researcher most often requires years of specialized training and extensive actual research experience.

The next step on the spectrum away from invested bystanders and toward researchers are those people who are making use of the educational system in order to learn. This group has more of a stake in the process than invested bystanders but their level of experience falls far short of needing to be actual researchers. This group, which most often consists of students and their parents (unless the students are adult students), we can call the *consumers* of education. This group is more concerned with the proper performance of educational systems than it is with how educational systems are designed, altered, and studied. The only time that educational research per se matters to them, usually, is in those situations where research (often new and controversial) plays a direct role in day-to-day education. Also, as consumers, they have the right to expect that the educational system will deliver on its promises and commitments, and these consumers have the right to hold educational systems accountable. Therefore, consumers are usually interested in the research process to the degree that research improves either the operation or accountability of education.

Before we leave the topic of consumers of education, it is only fair to point out that some educational researchers have defined teachers and administrators as consumers of educational research, as well (e.g., Hittleman & Simon, 2005; McMillan, 2011). We reject this notion explicitly and emphatically. It is our feeling that the notion of "consumer" implies a passive state of consumption, and there is nothing passive about the need of educational professionals for improving either their understanding or their engagement in the educational process. That is, they actively seek not just to be informed but also to be able to understand and engage in the results of the research they study. In other words, most professionals in education find themselves in between the consumers of research and the researchers themselves.

Those people whose skills and knowledge surpass those of the consumer, but who are not actual researchers themselves, we can call *research critics*. Research critics actively seek out research, and then engage critically in its findings.

The purpose of this book is to help you start down the road toward becoming an authentic research critic in the field of education. Here is our plan of action:

- In Chapter Two, we look at the basic levels of understanding that all research critics need to develop. These understandings deal with the nature of educational research per se, as well as an understanding of the quantitative approach to research, the use of statistics as both a perspective and a tool, the qualitative approach to research, and finally how mixed methods approaches might be developed and used.
- In Chapter Three, we make a case for why articles are the basis of research literacy, and then compare and contrast quantitative and qualitative articles.
- In Chapters Four through Eleven, we carefully and systematically examine each and every one of the key aspects of research article structure, from the title through Discussions and Conclusions. In this manner, we build our ongoing critical awareness of the purpose and role of each of these formal parts, and how they differ across qualitative and quantitative articles.
- In Chapter Twelve, we examine concepts where we will need to grow more experienced, and directions we can follow to build upon our growing expertise.
- In Chapter Thirteen, we conclude by looking at both the future and the bigger picture.

While some of this material might be challenging to you, we suspect that other parts will be quite familiar and straight-forward. We have chosen to err on the side of caution, to try to ensure that we are as clear as possible and that all of us are able to move forward together. We know that you are very intelligent and that you know a great deal about education and even educational research, but all of us are prone at times to gaps in our knowledge and understanding.

We invite you to move forward in the exciting process of developing your skills toward becoming a research critic.

Chapter Two

Basic Approaches in Educational Research

EDUCATIONAL RESEARCH IS BUILT upon an ongoing and evolving foundation of research articles. While there are books and monographs in our field, the majority of research is reported in article form. In fact, JSTOR lists some 477 journals devoted to the publishing of original research studies in education. Therefore, it makes perfectly good sense to master the basics of research articles in our attempt to become research literate in this field.

Before we look at articles themselves, however, we need to step back and take a look at the basic foundations of educational research itself.

Basics of Educational Research

Education is one of the most fundamental things that human beings do. In order for us to survive, from the most personal to the broadest cultural level, we need to be able to teach and learn from each other. When we talk about education, though, we are usually referring to some form of schooling.

Schooling consists of formal systems of teaching and learning, usually occurring within some specialized setting and employing specialized methods. The default model of schooling is a classroom, staffed by a teacher using a curriculum to guide instruction, with some form of ongoing assessment of student learning. From these default conditions we can lay out some of the key questions that drive educational research:

- What are the most important things for students to learn?
- What are students like, and how can we use this knowledge to improve the ways we teach them?
- How can we improve the learning process?
- How can we help teachers teach better?

In order to get at these and other important questions, we need to improve our understanding of the nature and application of research. That is, we need to become more research literate. To this end, we will take a brief look at the basics of quantitative literacy, statistical literacy, and qualitative literacy in turn.

The Quantitative Approach

When we talk about quantitative research, we are talking about research that follows the principles of the *scientific method*. There are many different formulations of the scientific method, but most of them share the following common principles:

- We make careful observations
- We make predictions from those observations
- We test those predictions
- We use our findings to support or modify our predictions

Beyond this bare bones understanding of the scientific method, there are a number of other major aspects of the quantitative approach. These other aspects allow us to see how the scientific method is crafted into a process that strives to examine the basic nature of the educational process. Toward this task, there are three directions, or guidelines, that are particularly important when putting together quantitative research in the field of education.

First of all, there is an emphasis on the typical. That is, when we do quantitative research, we are most often interested in how the typical student, for example, learns a typical lesson in a typical situation from a typical teacher. This is important because, if we understand the typical, we can then understand how most educational situations unfold. Once we have the basic framework, then all we need to do is fill in the particular details. Even if we find ourselves with an unusual situation, we can still compare that situation to what is typical.

Here are some examples of the sorts of typical things that we might look at in educational research:

- How many hours of homework the average high school student does each evening
- The number of hours of sleep these students get every evening and how it affects their grades
- The amount of grade point average improvement we tend to find when we do some kind of intervention with students

Secondly, we are looking for things that are regular and repeatable. We cannot make any predictions or create rules or laws from one-of-a-kind events. Ideally, not only are these sorts of things predictable but they are also controllable to some degree.

Here are some of the regular things we might look at within a program of educational research:

- Attitudes toward learning
- Degree of motivation for doing specific learning tasks
- Favorable or unfavorable opinions about teachers

Furthermore, here are some things that are both regular and controllable:

- Amount of time available to do homework
- Amount of nutrition both before and during school hours
- Specific instructions for doing learning tasks

Finally, our research must be public. We make our research public by reporting not only our findings but also the procedures we used to get them. These procedures include the exact research questions we asked, as well as a detailed account of the methods we used to answer those questions. These procedures should be reported in a clear and complete fashion, so that if someone wanted to repeat our exact study, they have enough information to do so.

Before we leave our discussion of the quantitative approach, we need to say a few words about variables. Anything that we can assign a value to is a measurement. For instance, we can measure height, weight, intelligence, and so on. Furthermore, there are two basic types of measurements—constants and variables. Constants are just what they sound like—measurements that do not change. It is rare in educational research to measure constants, usually because most of the important constants have already been identified and accounted for.

Variables are another matter. Variables are measurements that can change, either within people or across people. For instance, we can get older or taller or heavier or smarter. Measurements across people give us pictures of how a given group of people might vary on this kind of measurement. Both are important in educational research.

There is another important distinction to make when talking about the use of variables in educational research. That is the distinction between an *independent variable* and a *dependent variable*.

The logic is most often like this—we do something to the independent variable, and then we measure its impact on the dependent variable. For instance, we give children different kinds of food for breakfast (this is our independent variable) and then we look at how each group of kids performs on a math quiz (dependent variable).

Measuring variables is necessary for nearly all forms of quantitative research. Comparing variables is also extremely common. Manipulating independent variables and then seeing the impact on dependent variables is at the very heart of doing experiments.

The Nature of Statistics

Just about every quantitative article in education makes use of statistics, to one degree or another. We will not talk about actual statistical tests and techniques just yet, but we will save that discussion for how they are used to answer research questions (in the Results and Findings chapters). For now, we will look at a few of the basic concepts of statistics that are useful to keep in mind when we see statistical results.

Why are statistics so important for quantitative research? There are a number of key reasons:

- Statistics is a useful tool to use to describe our data
- Statistics is a useful tool to use to test our data
- Statistics is a powerful tool to use to model the nature and operation of the empirical world

Let us consider each of these key insights in turn.

Descriptive Statistics

The simplest use of statistics is to gather data and organize them in a meaningful way. When we do this, we are creating *distributions.*

A distribution is an assembly of related measurements that we combine to get a group picture. For instance, each and every one of us has a height, a weight, and various other measurable characteristics (like shoe size, arm length, and so on) and abilities (like a hundred-meter dash speed, IQ, recall ability from memory, and so on).

By themselves, our individual measures may or may not be that interesting. But if we combine our measures with other people who are similar to us in some clear and objective way (for instance, same age, same income level, same profession, and so on) we can begin to form a group picture that sheds more light on what we might expect from the average or typical person in our group.

In addition, these descriptive pictures tend to be more balanced and stable than any individual measure. Some of the more typical descriptive statistical concepts, such as the mean, median, mode, range, and standard deviation will be discussed in some detail when we look at quantitative results and findings.

We need to make one last point about distributions. There are any number of different distributions that have been identified and studied, such as the Poisson distribution or the F distribution or the t distribution, among others. But unless the researchers say otherwise, their variables will fall into a normal distribution (or, as is commonly stated, they will be normally distributed). This is because almost all naturally occurring variables, including the ones discussed above, are normally distributed. There are deep and important theoretical and methodological reasons for this fact, but they are beyond our scope of discussion here.

Inferential Statistics

The second primary function of statistics is to help us make decisions. To do this, we often make use of inferential statistics. This makes sense, since the term "inferential" is based on the notion of inference, or using reasoning skills to put together a decision based on available information.

The first thing to realize about inferential statistics is that all decisions are "yes/no" decisions. That is, when we are using inferential statistics, we are trying to decide whether two or more things are different from each other, or whether they are just different-looking cases of the same thing. This is most clearly illustrated when we look at some of the areas where we are seeking these kinds of "yes/no" decisions.

Inferences and Frequencies The first area deals with frequencies. When we compare frequencies of occurrence across two or more conditions, we try to decide if these frequencies are essentially the same for each condition. Because of the natural vagaries and whims of everyday life, we would not expect these frequencies to be identical. But, at some point, we decide that the differences are too great to be incidental. For instance, we might expect roughly the same number of men and women in the US Senate (there are one hundred senators, so this makes the math easier). In this case, our expected frequencies are 50 percent of each. If the actual frequencies were, say, 55 percent men and 45 percent women we would not think that is too far from our expectations. As we get to 60 percent men and 40 percent women we are less sure, but we are still willing to concede to chance. Currently, the frequency is about 80 percent men and 20 percent women. While this is far better than the not-so-distant past, where the figures were 98 percent men and 2 percent women, nonetheless we would not expect these numbers by chance alone (measured by a technique we call Chi-square analysis).

Inferences and Relationships The second kind of "yes/no" inference deals with deciding whether a given relationship is greater than we might expect by chance. When we are typically looking at variables that we can only measure but cannot control, we often correlate them (note that the term correlation has the concept of co-relation built into it). For instance, we can measure outside temperature in our hometown (which we cannot control, obviously) and compare the daily temperature to the number of pints of ice cream sold in the local grocery store (also not easy to control).

If there were actually no relation between these two variables, then we would expect them to go their merry ways, so to speak. But suppose we find that, in general, as the outside temperature rises the number of pints of ice cream sold increases. We would not expect a perfect correlation here, since folks often buy ice cream in the winter and abstain at times in the summer for reasons having nothing to do with the temperature outside. But we can use inferential statistical tools (in this case, a correlation coefficient) to determine that the joint rise and fall of these two variables is most likely not just a matter of chance.

Inferences and Hypotheses Our final inferential situation deals with deciding if common variables between two or more conditions act like one another, or whether at least one of those conditions seems to be acting differently. The simplest case of this involves a treatment and a control group. We do something different to the treatment group, and look to see if it has any impact on the target variable. That is, does the treatment group look different from the control group? For instance, suppose we divide a bunch of kids into two groups. We teach the first group how to make and read a simple code. The second group reads comic books just to keep them occupied. Then we give each kid a coded message and measure how long it takes each kid to solve the code. Of course we would expect some variability. Some kids like solving codes, or may be naturally better at it. But if we looked at each group and compared their times (using, in this case, a technique called the independent t-test) and found the code training group was overall faster at a level that would be hard to explain just by chance, then we have validated to some degree our code training methods.

Inferences and Probabilities In all of our inferential examples, we talked about whether a finding was significant or not. We need to clarify what that concept means methodologically.

Remember that we said that all inferences are "yes/no" inferences. In actuality, they are "probably yes/probably no" inferences. That is, we can never say with complete certainty that, say, a treatment group is different from a control group. That is because, when you are dealing with sampling, you cannot ever rule out the possibility that your results are due to a strange and highly unlikely sample.

A simple example should make this point clear. Suppose you tossed a coin and got twenty heads in a row. The odds of getting twenty heads in a row are 1,049,000 to 1. Does this mean your coin is unbalanced and will always land heads, or does it mean you have happened onto a really rare, but theoretically possible, sample? You solve this problem by putting some expectations on the probabilities you are willing to live with. In most studies, researchers are willing to live with circumstances where the possibility of a random rare sample occurring is either 20 to 1 or 100 to 1. In either case, the researchers are setting a critical value. At or below that value, you have a rare naturally occurring sample. Above that value, you are looking at two different populations. When you can claim that you are looking at two different populations, then your findings are *significant.*

In the case of the twenty heads in a row, you can say that this finding is significantly different from chance. This does not tell you why the findings are significantly different from chance, just that they are. Hopefully, you have thought out a reason ahead of time why this difference should exist.

When reporting significance, researchers indicate this by asterisking the computed value, and linking it to the pre-selected probability level. For a finding that is significant at the 20 to 1 level, it might look like this:

13.67*   *(p<.05), which means probability less than 5 percent

At the 100 to 1 level it might look like this:

13.67*   *(p<.01), which means probability less than 1 percent

There is one final probability concept that we need to address concerning inferences. This deals with the fact that the likelihood of an inference is sensitive to the number of measurements we have amassed. Here is a simplified example. Suppose we measure the IQ of two people and get an average IQ of one hundred. How confident are we that this average is correct? Now suppose we measure the IQ of a million people and get an average of one hundred. We are much more confident that our sample of a million people is more representative of the population as a whole than our sample of two people (even though, coincidently, we got the same estimate of the population from each sample). All of this goes to prove that at least in some settings, the size of our samples matters.

The most common method for incorporating sample sizes into our inferences is by the use of *degree of freedom*. A degree of freedom is a measure of the impact of the sample size on the likelihood of our inference. If our sample size consists of N cases, then most of the time the degree of freedom is (N-1). Researchers report degrees of freedom to let the readers know the size of the samples used to make inferences, and these sample sizes are used to adjust critical values. As a rule of thumb, the smaller the sample the larger the critical value has to be in order for the results to be significant at the selected probability level.

Statistical Modeling

The final, and in some ways most interesting, property of statistics is its ability to model many of the key aspects of the world of experience itself. There is both an immediate and a far-reaching side to statistical modeling.

At the immediate level, we see that improved theoretical and especially improved computational capabilities (fostered almost entirely by the growth and advancement of computers) have enhanced our ability to look at quite a few relevant variables at the same time. This allows us to tackle larger and more complex questions—no longer are we limited to looking at just one or two variables at a time. These modeling tools include such processes as multiple regressions, path analyses, cohort analyses, structural equation modeling, and many more. They all share the ability to work with a large number of variables at the same time in order to improve either our theoretical understanding, our predictive abilities, or most often both of these.

At the far end of statistical modeling, where we take a broader philosophical view of statistics and its role in describing the nature of the world, we come face-to-face with three profound insights about the interaction of research and reality.

First of all, there is the realization that human dynamics are so rich and complex that mere causal claims cannot do justice to (or completely capture) the crucial interactions we deal with in everyday life. For instance, there was once a belief that poverty caused crime. While it seems to be true that there are more reported and obvious crimes in poor neighborhoods, the picture is actually far more complicated. Many people in poverty lead honest and virtuous lives, and any number of middle-class and upper-class individuals commit crimes. Merely testing hypotheses is not enough, researchers realized. They needed to bring together many variables and look at their differential impacts on a number of different types of people dealing with different life situations. When we do this kind of research, we move beyond testing claims into modeling life impacts.

At an even deeper level, there is the further realization that no research project can completely and accurately capture every facet of what it is trying to study. Even the very act of measuring can change what we are measuring. Therefore, all data sets are actually approximations of what they purport to measure, and all claims made from these research efforts are probable rather than certain. The idea of refining research to the point where we have perfect studies is not just a practical impossibility, but a theoretical impossibility as well. Therefore, we will not be able to replace statistical findings with more perfect findings, since those more perfect findings cannot actually ever exist. So at this level, statistics is not just the best game in town—it is actually the only game in town.

This leads us to our last, and deepest, point. The reason that statistical pictures work so well as models of the world is that freedom is built into the very fabric of reality. That is, no matter how precise or mechanical a process is, it is never completely and totally determined. It exists merely along a continuum of freedom. When we are dealing with carefully configured phenomena, such as timepieces and airplane engines and the like, these variations from perfect determination are called errors. As we move toward more complex and organic phenomena, it begins to look more and more like choice and free will. But in reality it is the necessary presence of freedom, no matter how small or how rich and complex, that is woven into the fabric of reality. And to date, statistics is our best available language to talk about such panoramas of phenomena.

In summary, statistics takes us from being able to organize simple information to being able to describe and model complex and free-ranging phenomena, and all points in between. No wonder it is so important on the empirical research landscape.

The Qualitative Approach

As educational research continues to grow and develop, we would not be surprised to see that research in general becomes less and less restricted to only quantitative studies, but that qualitative research comes to grow and flourish and to establish its own important identity within this domain. But before we consider these possibilities, we need to take a closer look at the qualitative approach in general.

The qualitative perspective takes its own approach to the process of doing educational research. Where quantitative research is concerned with measuring, predicting, and controlling, qualitative research is concerned with exploring, digging deeper, and understanding what things mean. So for our purposes here, rather than thinking of these two approaches as being end points of a continuum, it is much more useful to think of them as being mostly independent of each other. In that way, you can look at each of them on their own terms.

Defining Characteristics of Qualitative Research

Qualitative research, because it is a much younger discipline, has less of a history of theoretical development. As a consequence, more often than not it is defined by its methods and perspectives. There are, however, at least a few defining characteristics. Some of the most important are described here.

Targeting Meaning over Facts Qualitative research has been defined as a systematic empirical inquiry into meaning (Shank, 2005). By this, we see that qualitative research assumes that the world is always meaning-rich. Too often in our research culture we assume the opposite—that there is not enough meaning in the world and therefore that the world is meaning-poor. From a quantitative perspective, we try to fix this situation by adding more information, with the assumption that increasing information increases meaningfulness.

To move away from this "poverty" model into a richer picture of meaning is one of the key aims of qualitative research. We can see this particularly clearly when we look at the ways that human beings tend to operate together to address common goals.

For instance, we might know very little about how people form quilting societies in order to address their common interests and desires to do quilting. But as we come to look at quilting societies, and observe and talk to the quilters who are there on a regular basis over the years, we come to find a richer picture of this "world," a world that we might once have assumed to be fairly simple and straightforward. Finding areas of depth like this within the boundaries of educational practice is one of the most exciting aspects of qualitative research in education.

Focusing on Understanding over Knowing If you are looking at the world of experience first and foremost as a source of meaning, then the process of understanding becomes your primary goal. That is, if meaning is the coin of the realm, then understanding is its payoff. More often than not, such understandings take the form of insights, where our picture of things has been illuminated, and we receive deeper and richer insights into what might have seemed to be more mundane to us at one time.

Going back to our example of quilting societies, it is important for us to understand what quilting means to these participants. Quite often, we are surprised and even delighted to discover insights that cause us to look at quilting, and maybe even learning, in different ways.

Looking at Differences in Kind Instead of Differences in Degree In many quantitative studies, there are circumstances that are either known or hypothesized to be important. For instance, we all assume that proper sleep is important for school children. Therefore, we tend to ask such questions as: How much sleep do kids need? What happens when they get too little, or too much sleep? These are examples of what we mean by differences *in degree*. We all agree that sleep is important, but we don't know yet to what degree we need it.

Qualitative researchers tend to look at different types of change—what happens when things change and a person's world is no longer the same? These are differences *in kind*. That is, we become different kinds of people from one situation to the next. Differences in kind are also important when we look at other cultures and their traditions. That is, qualitative research acknowledges that cultural differences are not just in terms of the degree to which certain things are present or absent, but in how different cultures valorize different kinds of things and actions, and ignore others that we or others might deem important.

Key Qualitative Methods

As we said earlier, qualitative methods tend to play a crucial role in defining the conduct of given qualitative studies in education. The seven key methodological tools are as follows:

Observations This is the simple but powerful process of paying careful attention and documenting what you find when you do so. It is hard to imagine any sort of qualitative research that does not have some form of observational component.

Interviews How do you know what people think and believe? Often, the best way to find out is to ask them. There is a range of interview protocols, from the structured interview at one end, the semi-structured interview in the middle, and the unstructured interview at the other end. All three forms have their appropriate uses and places.

Focus Groups Focus groups had their beginnings in group therapy, where therapists realized that when people collectively address a topic or problem, this process often brings out insights and ideas that might have eluded us individually. Focus groups play important roles in areas as diverse as research and marketing, and have evolved into a process that uses clear and sophisticated rules.

Material Analysis Human beings tend to make and use things. The collective total of these things for a group is called its material record or culture. This material culture can tell us much about those who build and prize it, and includes both important formal things (like church buildings and historical monuments and great novels and movies) to things that are more informal and ephemeral (like comic books and baseball cards).

Archive and Historical Records Analysis Most societies and cultures keep records and retain information of historical significance. These archives and records can be rich sources of information, insight, and meaning.

Interpretive Analysis Often called hermeneutics, this method involves the careful "reading" of not only texts, but also customs, patterns of behavior, habits, celebrations, rituals, and the like. These "reading" processes are used to dig under the surface, and to look for connections to areas that on the surface might appear to be unrelated.

Participant Observation Participant observation occurs when researchers join into the lives and activities of those people they are studying, often with the intent of improving the lives of those they are working with.

Qualitative Methodological Perspectives

Finally, we need to take a look at how these various qualitative characteristics and tools are brought together to form important methodological perspectives. Each of these perspectives has a rich and nuanced history of practice. The seven basic methodological perspectives are as follows:

Ethnography Ethnography is the oldest method practiced by qualitative researchers. Ethnographers immerse themselves in a given culture, to try to understand the customs, beliefs, and day-to-day activities of that culture. In the early days, ethnographers went to remote and unstudied locales to work with little-known peoples. Nowadays, ethnographers often work in familiar areas like schools and suburban neighborhoods. A special type of ethnography is called autoethnography, where ethnographers study their own backgrounds and reactions.

Grounded Theory Grounded theory is a form of qualitative research pioneered in the 1960s by Glaser and Strauss, who were medical sociologists. In grounded theory, researchers set aside their preconceptions and use directed observation to find important themes that can be used to create theoretical perspectives. Grounded theory bills itself as a bottom-up process and is still quite influential today.

Case Studies When researchers do case studies, they concentrate on just a few persons, and most often just one person. Often, people who are extraordinary in their fields are targeted for the close-up look that case study research allows for.

Narrative Analysis Human beings are narrative creatures, and we routinely constitute our vision of the world via story. Qualitative researchers often use tools for parsing and understanding narratives that have been developed by sociolinguistic researchers and comparative literary critics. Chief among these tools is discourse analysis, which allows us to look carefully at multiple dimensions of the spoken word.

Oral Histories In many ways, oral historians are special types of ethnographers. Most often, researchers go into remote areas or talk with marginalized people in order to secure an oral record of accounts and beliefs and understandings that might otherwise get lost.

Critical Theory Critical theorists believe that certain ideological perspectives can be powerfully applied to the study of settings where there are social, economic, or cultural power imbalances. In particular, critical theorists most often look to use their theoretical tools to expose hidden areas of oppression and intimidation. Some of the main critical theories are based on a sophisticated application of an analysis of the roles of gender, race, or economics.

Action Research Action research was born in the work of Marxist researchers during the 1930s, and the pioneering work of Paulo Freire in the 1950s and 1960s in Brazil. Action research is based on the notion that it is not enough to just study some situation; you need to make things better by the time you leave. Action researchers often work with marginalized persons in marginal settings.

The Mixed Methods Approach

So far, we have been talking (at least from a teaching perspective) as if qualitative and quantitative approaches are essentially independent of each other. We should hasten to note that this is far from a settled matter. In fact, there are two camps in the educational research community regarding the relationship of these two modes to each other.

The approach that we call the *independent* perspective says that the power in the assumption that qualitative and quantitative approaches are independent of each other is in the ability to ask completely different *types* of research questions, depending on which approach you use. Therefore, there is always the very real possibility that a research question asked from one perspective will literally not make sense from the other perspective (Shank, 2005). It also follows that if these approaches are independent, and often at cross-purposes with each other, then it makes no sense to talk of mixed methods research.

There are a great many other educational researchers who hold a completely different position. They are adherents of what we can call the *global* approach to research. This global perspective says that research is research—and that the type of research is far less important than the questions asked. This perspective tends to hold that the most important thing about research is the research questions that are asked, and that the choice of method should only be made once the research question itself is clear. Furthermore, it tends to assume that while most research questions are best served by using one approach over another, in principle it makes sense to assume that the question could be answered to some degree or another by either of the approaches.

From the global perspective, mixed methods articles make sense in those situations where the research question requires both a qualitative and a quantitative approach to the problem. The reason that these approaches can be mixed is that, at heart, they are both scientific and use, in their own fashions, the scientific method. Remember, these claims, while they seem plausible on the surface, are far from settled.

It follows, then, that mixed methods articles fall within the framework of the global perspective. Even so, it is highly unlikely that both approaches are evenly represented in a given study. For our purposes, there are two broad types of mixed methods articles:

- **Quantitative-leading.** In a quantitative-leading article, the basic design is quantitative. Often, there are relationships or hypotheses tested. The qualitative component is used to elaborate on the findings and to help create a richer description and interpretation of the data. This is the most common form of mixed methods article.
- **Qualitative-leading.** This is the less common form of mixed methods article. Quantitative data, mostly descriptive, are brought in to clarify the parameters of the study. That is, we are given basic demographic information about the people and settings that are being examined. In some cases, relationships are explored. Finally, in some participative action research studies, quantitative measures are used to test the effectiveness of the studies.

The question of whether quantitative and qualitative approaches are independent will take many years to settle. In the meantime, we are ready to look at how quantitative and qualitative approaches are used to create basic types of quantitative and qualitative articles. This is the focus of the next chapter.

Chapter Three

Types of Research Articles

THERE ARE TWO FUNDAMENTAL types of research articles in education—quantitative articles and qualitative articles. We will look at each type in turn.

Types of Quantitative Articles

Of the two article types, quantitative articles have been around longer and are probably more common. While many journals publish both types of articles, there are some journals that only publish quantitative articles.

There are two key issues to look at here—what is the basic formal structure of a quantitative article, and what sorts of research agendas can we expect from such articles?

Quantitative Article Formats

Quantitative articles tend to have the following basic form:

- Title
- Names and Institutional Homes of the Researchers
- Abstract
- Introduction (sometimes not labeled as such)

- Methods (or Procedures)
- Results (or Findings)
- Discussion (or Conclusions)
- References

Each of these areas will be discussed in detail in upcoming chapters. For now, it is important for you to see how common this basic form really is. When you are aware of this form, then it allows you to group and organize the article before you actually know what it is about. In other words, if you understand the *form* of the article, then you are better prepared to understand its *contents*.

Quantitative Article Research Agendas

Once you understand basic format points, it is then important to understand the types of work that quantitative articles most often do. Each quantitative article does one or more of the following:

Organize Data The more carefully researchers can organize their information, the clearer the statements they can then make. There are a variety of ways that information can be organized:

- Tables allow for clear organization of what often ends up as a large array of data.
- Graphs and charts allow readers to get a visual take on certain patterns.
- Basic demographic information about samples, such as means and standard deviations, allows researchers to depict how certain data tend to form distributions.
- Reports of frequencies for certain occurrences are useful for allowing researchers to see how common or uncommon certain events are.

Researchers carefully select and apply these kinds of organizational strategies to their findings, depending on the nature of the research itself. But nearly every quantitative study is improved by good data organization.

Discover and Examine Relationships Finding and organizing relevant data are very important, but most quantitative research articles push further in a number of other directions. One key direction is the exploration of possible relationships among key variables. When researchers can show that variables are linked together in systematic ways, then they can begin to understand important things via these relationships. For instance, if researchers can show that hunger and poor grades are clearly linked, then this can open up numerous avenues for research that can explore this potential relationship between nutrition and learning.

Test Hypotheses Finding relationships is an important task for researchers, but it then becomes even more important to determine, if possible, just how such relationships work in controllable and predictable ways. To do this, researchers need to create and test hypotheses. Most of the time, a hypothesis is an educated guess concerning which variables might cause changes in other variables. To be a worthwhile hypothesis, these guesses need to be testable. When this happens, the researchers can then make some powerful causal claims about the relationships. For instance, if some students are allowed to use calculators and other students have to compute answers by hand, researchers can claim that calculator use causes students to get more correct computations if there is a significant improvement for the calculator group. This is a much stronger claim than just to say that better computational skills seem to be related to calculator use.

Build Models As researchers got better and better at finding and testing simple relationships and hypotheses, they became emboldened in tackling more complex issues. This makes perfectly good sense, since most educational situations and activities are naturally quite complex. And as cheaper and more powerful computers came onto the scene, researchers also had the tools they needed to make more complicated and massive computations. As a result, statistical modeling has become more and more important in educational research. Researchers can now sort out the impact of literally dozens of variables, if need be, on their targeted behaviors. For instance, researchers can look at the relative impacts that such variables as gender, standardized test scores, extracurricular activities, socioeconomic status, number of siblings, afterschool work, and so on, have on how well a high school student might do in college.

Types of Qualitative Articles

Qualitative research is a fairly new area for educational articles. Qualitative articles are sometimes published in journals that publish both types of articles, but more than quantitative work, there are a number of journals that explicitly publish qualitative research. For instance, you will find only qualitative articles in a journal like *Qualitative Inquiry* or *Qualitative Reports* or *Qualitative Research in Education*.

There are two key topics to look at here—what is the basic formal structure of a qualitative article, and what sorts of work can we expect from such articles?

Qualitative Article Formats

Qualitative articles tend to have less structured formats than quantitative articles. The actual format of the article depends heavily on the methods used. Ethnographies and case studies, for instance, tend to use more narrative accounts, while grounded theories and critical theory articles tend to be more formal and more structured along the lines of quantitative articles.

Qualitative Article Research Agendas

Like quantitative articles, qualitative articles have a range of things they are trying to accomplish. In general, most qualitative articles target one or more of the following activities:

Discovering Meaning In many cases, qualitative researchers are interested in looking at circumstances and situations that are not well understood. Rather than look for patterns among variables or testing hypotheses, they decide to go back to ground zero and look at the situation with fresh eyes. That is, it is not so much a case of having a wrong understanding as it is a case of not having a rich enough understanding in the first place. By working on building and enhancing these sorts of understandings in poorly explored settings, researchers can follow the trail until things start looking clearer and new perspectives come into focus. By crafting these sorts of enhanced understandings, without following any specific theoretical trail, new avenues of research are often uncovered.

Investigating Meaning One common goal of qualitative research is to try to understand perplexing situations. There are two primary ways to do this. The first approach is by digging into the matter at hand. Suppose we find out that there is one particular middle school math class that is seriously outperforming all other middle school math classes in its district. Why is this? The qualitative researcher might act like a detective and start investigating the situation, looking for clues as to what is happening to cause this class to distinguish itself from others. It is important that researchers, in this situation, take their time to try to come up with explanations. The longer they dig, and the more patient they are with the process, the more likely they are to find some deep and subtle aspect of the situation that has eluded previous researchers.

Illuminating Understanding The second way to look at perplexing situations is to take a look at the basic assumptions and perspectives that we hold toward those situations in the first place. Sometimes, when we shift perspectives, whole new avenues for understanding open up as a result. For instance, suppose we shift from looking at schools as places where learning is created (or a manufacturing approach) to places where learning is nurtured or grown (this is not so far-fetched—in German, kindergarten means "child garden"). When a focus for understanding is shifted, then who knows what sorts of new insights might follow?

Making Things Better When articles talk about making things better, they are generally reporting on some form of participatory action research. In participatory action research, the researchers strive to become a part of the solution. For instance, researchers might work with parents to create a stronger community outreach program, or with teachers to enhance and streamline school governance. The quantitative model of being the passive observer is put aside in favor of being an active agent for improvement.

Conclusions

At this point, we have developed a clear and comprehensive framework for understanding educational research articles. By looking at both quantitative and qualitative approaches, and the ways these approaches often get translated in the formal structure of articles, we have created a broader overall picture of research articles in operation. For the next several chapters, we will look at each and every major aspect of educational research articles, point by point. In this fashion, we will be taking our broad understanding and applying it to the nuts and bolts details of what goes into making up an educational research article.

Chapter Four

Understanding Titles
and Abstracts

LET'S BEGIN THE PROCESS of looking at educational research articles part by part.

The first two things you will read in every educational research article will be the *title* of the article and (very often) its Abstract. We will start our critical step-by-step analysis of the research article by looking at these two key components.

The Title

Every research article has a title. When it is well done, the title is a concise and clear introduction to the article. Unless the researchers are being deliberately clever or enticing, the title will almost always give you some immediate sense of what the article is about. That is, it is best to be straightforward and direct.

One way to understand what a title might tell us is for us to understand what type of title it is. When we identify the title type, this gives us some early and important information about what type of article we are going to read. For our purposes, there are five basic title types.

The Situation Title

In many ways, this is the simplest title type. As this label suggests, the title is describing a given situation. Here are a few fictional examples:

- Patterns of Afterschool Involvement for Children of Undocumented Immigrants
- Internet Use by High School Students in Rural Libraries
- Comparing High Stakes Standardized Test Results across Time Zones

As you can see in each of these examples, often we are looking at particular activities or particular populations or both. Situation titles also often describe research where we tend to observe, rather than control, the key variables of interest.

The Process Title

When we have a situation title, we are describing an ongoing state of affairs. With the process title, we are talking about something that is either happening that we are directly involved in, or something that we intend to make happen. That is, we are either observing or implementing a process. Here are a few fictional examples:

- Exploring Strategies for Teaching Economic Literacy to Children in Poverty
- Comparing Physical Fitness and Academic Approaches to Afterschool Care
- Increasing Parental Involvement in Upper-Middle-Class Neighborhoods

When researchers use process titles, they are much more likely to be talking about research efforts where they are able to exert some form of influence or control. At the same time, they are often looking at broad and comprehensive educational or social patterns as well. That is why process titles can be found equally in use with qualitative or quantitative articles.

The Equation Title

Perhaps the most common title type is what we will call the equation title. This type of title is most common in quantitative articles. Here are a few fictional examples:

- The Impact of Sleep Deprivation on Short-Term Memory Retention
- Parental Neglect as a Factor in School Absenteeism
- The Effect of Gamma Rays on Man-in-the-Moon Marigolds (with Apologies to David Mamet)

We call these types of titles equation titles because you can often use these titles to sit down and write out equations to describe the key variables of the study and their relations to each other. Because the discovery of relationships and the testing of hypotheses is such a large part of educational research, it is no surprise that equation titles are so common.

The Theoretical Title

This is a much less common title type than the previous three types. When we have a theoretical title, the theory is the key element of the research article. Here are a few fictional examples:

- School Violence and Maslow's Hierarchy of Needs: Some Empirical Trends
- Testing Piaget's Conservation of Mass in Young Children in Southeast Asia
- Locus of Control Effects in Studying for Standardized Tests

When researchers use a theoretical title, they are not just interested in looking at some phenomenon, but how that target of study relates to some larger or more abstract theoretical area. Often, theoretical titles are found when researchers are building a body of work whose findings are all related to some key theoretical perspective.

The Indirect Title

We will finish with what is by far the most uncommon title type—the indirect title. Indirect titles are designed to raise our interest without necessarily telling us much about the contents of the article. For instance, here is a fictional example of an indirect title:

Giving the Devil His Due

This title tells us something about how the researchers feel about the topic or situation, to some degree, but we do not know what that topic or situation actually is. In almost every case of an indirect title, we will find a qualifying phrase to point us toward the topic or situation:

Giving the Devil His Due: Working with the Causes of Delinquency in Middle Schools

In this case, and in the case of almost all indirect titles, the qualifying phrase is, itself, capable of acting as a stand-alone title. In this case, we can see that it would be a process title.

Using Title Types Wisely

Before we leave this discussion on titles and what they can tell us, we need to make a few summary points.

First of all, identifying title types is far from an exact science. Sometimes it is hard to distinguish between one or more choices. That is why it is always best to think of title typing as a general way to anticipate the nature of a study. For instance, if it is an equation title, then the article is less likely to be qualitative.

Secondly, applying title types should always be done to make your work easier, not harder. If you find yourself agonizing over which choice to make, you are working too hard. Relax and see what the title is trying to tell you.

Finally, typing the title is only one step in the overall process of engaging critically in the article. If, after reading and thinking about the article for a while, you think it is a good idea to shift to a different title type, then by all means do so. Again, the entire process of critical reading is designed to make things clearer, not to muddy the waters.

The Abstract

After the title, more often than not we find an Abstract. There are many different ways to do an Abstract. The most common Abstract format in educational research is APA format, or the format prescribed by the *Publication Manual of the American Psychological Association*.

A good abstract is 100 to 250 words long. In general, a good abstract

- Provides an overview of the article itself
- Addresses how and why the research was done
- Summarizes key findings

Furthermore, a good abstract often

- Describes the research participants and setting
- Clearly states the purpose of the research
- Specifies the type of analysis used
- Summarizes key conclusions

As you can see, an Abstract has a lot of work to do in a very small space, using very few words. It has to be concise, because its purpose is to provide a quick summary of the research article for readers who may or may not wish to read further.

Often, the decision to read further is affected by the content of the Abstract itself.

Because of the very few words allowed in the Abstract, there has evolved an informal process for writing Abstracts. Most of the time, one or more of the following points will be covered explicitly in a given Abstract. They are presented here in alphabetical order:

- Analysis
- Conclusions
- Design
- Participants
- Problem
- Purpose
- Results

Coding the Abstract

We will now look at two examples of Abstracts, and using the seven points above, we will learn how to code these Abstracts. The purpose of this coding is to allow us to make sure that we have identified all of the pertinent types of information within the Abstract.

The first example is a fictional example of a fairly standard sort of Abstract.

Standard Abstract

The purpose of this study was to examine whether online tutoring programs improve standardized math test scores for eighth graders. 210 students were recruited from a large midwestern city school district. Students were randomly assigned to an online tutoring group, a traditional tutoring group, or a control group. A repeated measures ANOVA was used to test for pre- and post-findings. Results show that both tutoring groups did better on the standardized tests than the control group, but there were no differences between the two tutoring conditions. These results suggest that online tutoring is at least as effective as face-to-face tutoring.

This abstract is fairly straightforward. In a little over one hundred words, it describes the main aspects of the study. Here is how it might be coded:

[PURPOSE] *The purpose of this study was to examine* [PROBLEM] *whether online tutoring programs improve standardized math test scores for eighth graders.* [PARTICIPANTS] *210 students were recruited from a large midwestern city school district.* [DESIGN] *Students were randomly assigned to an online tutoring group, a traditional tutoring group, or a control group.* [ANALYSIS] *A repeated measures ANOVA was used to test for pre- and post-findings.* [RESULTS] *Results show that both tutoring groups did better on the standardized tests than the control group, but there were no differences between the two tutoring conditions.* [CONCLUSIONS] *These results suggest that online tutoring is at least as effective as face-to-face tutoring.*

In this example, each of the seven primary abstract criteria was used, and was used only one time. Other abstracts can be a bit more unorthodox. This second fictional example illustrates this point.

Less Typical Abstract

Many teenagers feel that they learn better when they are allowed to use social media with each other to help check and correct their homework assignments. Given the newness of social media within education, this claim remains unproven. In this study, we worked with one hundred teens, randomly assigned to one of two groups. The first group worked in ten teams of five after school in study groups. The second group formed ten teams of five via Facebook. When homework scores were compared after a semester of working together, the Facebook groups did significantly better. Interviews revealed the teens in the Facebook group had more fun and worked together more hours. Follow-up research is needed to see if these trends persist over longer periods of time.

In this Abstract, the researchers are more concerned with getting out key points to their readers than in conforming to a particular format. We can see this when we code the Abstract:

[PARTICIPANTS] *Many teenagers* [PROBLEM] *feel that they learn better when they are allowed to use social media with each other to help check and correct their homework assignments.* [PURPOSE] *Given the newness of social media within education, this claim remains unproven. In this study, we worked with* [PARTICIPANTS] *one hundred teens,* [DESIGN] *randomly assigned to one of two groups.* [DESIGN] *The first group worked in ten teams of five after school in study groups. The second group formed ten teams of five via Facebook.* [RESULTS] *When homework scores were compared after a semester of working together, the Facebook groups did significantly better.* [RESULTS] *Interviews revealed the teens in the Facebook group had more fun and worked together more hours.* [CONCLU-SIONS] *Follow-up research is needed to see if these trends persist over longer periods of time.*

While this second Abstract shares many of the same components as the first Abstract, there are some basic differences. First of all, not all the components are present in the second Abstract—there is no explicit discussion of Analysis. Secondly, the order of presentation of the components is different. In the case of the second Abstract, the researchers most likely want to lead out with a discussion of their target audience and their concerns. Finally, some of the components are presented not all at once, but spread out over the Abstract as a whole. This was most likely done to help the reader understand how the article was going to treat these key issues.

Conclusions

In the next several chapters, we will move past the title and Abstract to look at various introductory components. We will start by looking for the *purposes* and *rationales* that the researchers give, either implicitly or explicitly, for doing the research in the first place.

Chapter Five

Understanding Purposes and Rationales

You have taken a close-up look at the roles of both the title and the Abstract. What is the next area for you to consider?

After the title and the Abstract, most likely you will find the Introduction. Sometimes the Introduction is labeled as such, but it is not uncommon to go right from the Abstract into the body of the article. That part of the article, after the Abstract up to the Methods section (sometimes called the Procedures section), is the Introduction.

The Introduction consists of a number of parts—the *rationale*, the *purpose*, the *research question*, and the *argument*. In many ways, the Introduction is the most important part of the article. If the Introduction is clear and well organized, all of the other sections of the article will flow naturally from it. That is why we need to spend time understanding the nature and function of the Introduction.

In this chapter, we will look at *purposes* and *rationales*. Researchers do their research because it matters to them. That is, there is always a purpose and a rationale for what they do. Furthermore, it is important that we, as readers, understand why this research is being done. That way, we can make sure that we are on the same wavelength as the researchers, whether we ultimately agree with them or not.

Types of Purposes

More often than not, researchers will not explicitly identify the purpose of the article as such. Instead, they will talk about what they are trying to accomplish with the research.

Overall, there are four general types of purposes that we can identify.

Exploration

When we find an *exploration* purpose, it is usually the case that the researchers are working in an area where things are often sketchy or poorly understood. Here is a fictional example of how a researcher might identify an exploration purpose:

> Bullying has historically been a face-to-face phenomenon. With the growth of the Internet, however, especially among school-age children, there has been a growing trend of cyberbullying. Because this phenomenon is so new, very little is known about it. That is the main reason we are looking at cyberbullying in this study.

Extension

The notion of the *extension* purpose is based on the realization that educational research is a collective process, and that studies often build on other studies. An extension purpose is found when researchers explicitly state that they are building on earlier work, either theirs or others'. Here is a fictional example of how researchers might frame an extension purpose:

A number of researchers (Alpha, 2008; Beta & Gamma, 2009; Delta, Epilson & Mu, 2010) have established that good sleep habits can improve early reading skill learning among preschoolers. All of these researchers assumed that eight hours is the proper amount of sleep for preschool children. But emerging research by Theta (2013) suggests that these children might optimally need ten hours of sleep. In this study, we are looking at how these extended recommended hours of sleep might be used to modify earlier findings.

Expansion

Expansion occurs when researchers are not just building on earlier work, but are attempting to extend the work into new or complex areas. Here is a fictional example of how researchers might frame an expansion purpose:

> Mu and Nu (2011), in their extensive review of the literature, have shown that problem-based learning is highly effective in teaching algebra concepts. This study examines more visually based modes of mathematical thinking, and in particular geometric thinking, to see if problem-based learning can be effective in this different realm of mathematical reasoning.

Correction

Sometimes, earlier research turns out to be wrong, for a variety of reasons. *Correction* occurs when researchers attempt to set the record straight with the current article. Here is a fictional example of how researchers might frame a correction purpose:

> School violence, particularly in poorer neighborhoods, has often been linked to poverty. But closer examination

over the years has shown that poverty, in and of itself, is not adequate to explain violence. Instead, other mitigating factors have been examined, with mixed results. In particular, depression was looked at early on, and then rejected. But there is evidence to suggest that these earlier measures of depression were not subtle enough to pick up the violence-related aspects of depression. Armed with newer and more sophisticated measures of depression, this study seeks to see if depression does play a key role in violence in schools in poor neighborhoods, after all.

Types of Rationales

Unlike the purpose, where the researchers address the role of their article within the overall educational research community, the rationale addresses the role of the article in the context of the larger educational community. That is, how does the article answer the larger "So What?" question that compels us to pay attention to what it is trying to accomplish?

Overall, there are five different basic rationales that researchers often attempt to address.

Crisis

The *crisis* rationale argues that the research is important because it looks at an area of crisis within either education or society as a whole. That is, something must change or we will be in trouble. This is a fairly evident "So What," so long as the researchers make their case.

Here is a fictional example of a crisis rationale:

Over the past decade, the so-called Digital Divide between the rich and poor in education has grown wider and wider. If this gulf continues to grow, it will most likely threaten the existence of education as we know it. Therefore, research on how to address and narrow the Digital Divide is critically important.

Importance

When we are dealing with an *importance* rationale, the rhetoric is a bit cooler and more analytic. The situation is not a crisis per se, but it is an important matter to address and one that the researchers feel that the field should not ignore. Sometimes, topics are so ingrained in our understanding of the current landscape of education and research that the researchers do not feel that it is necessary to do anything more than to identify the topic of the research. More often than not, though, the researchers need to make some case for the "So What" importance of their work.

Here is a fictional example of an importance rationale:

> Environmental education has grown more and more important over the years, particularly as issues like climate change continue to be debated. But what concepts are most important, particularly to introduce to younger children?

Gap-Filling

In the case of the *gap-filling* rationale, the "So What" factor addresses the growing body of research on the topic in question. Given that the topic is already accepted as important to the field, gap-filling goes on to do just that—fill in gaps of knowledge.

Here is a fictional example of a gap-filling rationale:

> The relationship between self-image and reading skills has been well documented for young children and has been shown to play a key role in career success for adults. However, the relationship between developing higher order reading skills and emerging self-image and life goals has

not been well studied in adolescents. This study seeks to address that gap.

Depth

Depth rationales have most often been associated with qualitative research. There, researchers often make a case for why it is important to look at their topic of focus in greater depth, as well as making the "So What" case for looking at the topic in the first place.

Here is a fictional example of a depth rationale:

> School lunch workers are usually considered to be merely an ancillary part of any given school. That is, they are there to dispense food to the students. But do they play other, often overlooked roles as well? To what extent do at least some of them act as advisors, confidants, or even role models for students? This is an area that deserves a closer look.

Commitment

A *commitment* rationale is also usually related to qualitative research, and is furthermore almost always associated with participatory action research. With this sort of rationale, the key area of inequity is explained, along with the reasons why this sort of research is the best way to approach the matter.

Here is a fictional example of a commitment rationale:

> The Huron school district (not its real name) has been on the verge of closure by the state for at least two decades. Dropping enrollments and dropping test scores, coupled with decreasing resources, have put this district on the verge of extinction. We were approached by the Huron school board to see if we could mount one last-ditch community effort to rescue the district. Given that one of the researchers was a student at this district many years ago, we were eager to take on this challenge. Furthermore, this

also gave us the platform to try out strategies that, so far, had only been evaluated theoretically.

Conclusions

It is valuable for us, as research critics, to be able to contextualize articles as we read them. That is why we need to pay attention to the purposes and rationales of the researchers. When we have a clear picture of the rationales involved, then we can decide whether those issues are important to us, as well. And one of the added benefits of understanding the purposes of an article is the fact that these purposes should point us directly to the research questions that were explored.

This leads us to the next chapter, where we look at the research questions and the arguments used to support them.

Chapter Six

Understanding Questions and Arguments

IN ORDER FOR A research study to exist, there needs to be at least one *research question* to be addressed. Once there has been a research question or questions established, then it is important to justify that question(s). This is where the *argument* comes in. The argument can take a number of forms. Finally, there is also a need to ground both the question and the argument within the existing research community. This is where the References come into play. In this chapter, we will look at the research question and the argument. In the next chapter, we will break the flow of the article, after a fashion, to jump to the end to look at the References.

Finding the Research Question(s)

Because the research question(s) is so important, it should be easy to find. That is, the researchers are obligated to make the research question(s) clear and explicit. Here is an example of a well-stated research question:

In this study, the following research question will be addressed: Does increasing study time for weekly math quizzes for third graders increase the number of correct answers on these quizzes?

When there is more than one research question, they are often listed like this:

The following research questions are proposed:

- Does environmental education increase the likelihood of recycling in classrooms?
- Does environmental education increase the likelihood of recycling in the school as a whole?
- Does environmental education increase the likelihood of recycling in students' homes?

Sometimes, the research question is stated clearly, but is not identified explicitly as such:

Third graders are often disorganized and inefficient in their use of study time. If they were taught more efficient ways to use that time, would it increase their test scores?

Sometimes, multiple research questions are listed less formally. In this sequence, three research questions are introduced, but in a narrative context:

One of the goals of environmental education is to increase recycling at a number of levels. At the most basic level, we hypothesize that an immediate impact of environmental education would be an increase in recycling in the classrooms that are learning proper environmental behavior. But this impact could be far wider. For instance, would we find that teaching environmental education might branch out and improve recycling for the school as a whole? And what is the likelihood that these students might take their recycling behaviors home and improve recycling in their family settings?

Finally, it is important to address the problem of a bad research question. There are a number of things that can make a research question bad:

- It is hard to find
- It is not stated clearly
- It cannot be properly tested
- It is a statement of opinion rather than a question

If you have read the introductory section of an article, and you have reached a discussion of Methods without having a clear notion of what is being addressed or tested, then you have a case of a "hard to find" question.

Here is an example of a research question that is not stated clearly because of the inclusion of irrelevant detail, opinion, and a vague statement of what the researchers want to address:

Because of their developmental level, third graders are often prone to socializing at their desks and gossiping about each other. This can be a great distraction to the teachers and other students alike. Why are they not more organized? Do they really want to study? Teachers note that such conditions make it difficult for some or all of their students to do well on tests. Can this be changed?

Here is a research question that cannot be properly tested because it is more of a matter of opinion:

Students want to recycle. That is because all of us want to recycle, because we all want to protect the planet. So if we teach them proper recycling procedures, will they become the environmental leaders of the twenty-first century?

While we have given you examples of bad research questions, it is not likely that you will see anything this blatant in published research articles. Nearly all of the time, the peer review process will eliminate articles that ask such bad questions. But if you progress in your career to the point where you are asked to review articles for publication, there is a very good chance you will read your fair share of bad or even non-existent research questions. Unfortunately, it is more common than you might suspect.

The Nature of the Argument

It is not enough just to state a research question. It needs to be justified. That is where the argument comes in. Both the research question and the argument can be found in the first part of the article. This is the part of the article between the title and the Abstract on one hand, and the Methods section on the other hand. Without an argument to support it, the research question is just a claim. Why is the question important? How can we justify asking and examining this particular research question? What sort of context do we have to have in order to see where the researchers are coming from? Does the research question make any sense? These are the sorts of questions that the argument addresses.

There are a few general principles that all arguments should exhibit:

- The argument should be clear
- The argument should be logical
- The argument should make a case for the research question(s)

If any of these criteria are missing, then there are potential problems with the argument.

Categorizing the Argument

Let us consider the following simple research question:

Do calculators help students do math word problems?

It is not clear and obvious why researchers might ask this question. They need to build a case for asking it. That is the main reason for putting together an argument.

Regardless of the actual content of the argument, there are only three forms that the argument can take. We can categorize these three forms in the following manner.

The Setup Argument

This is probably the most common form of research argument. When the researchers use a *setup argument*, they are concerned with building a case before they introduce the research question. That is, the researchers do not want to actually state the research question until they have explained to us why the question is important, where it comes from conceptually, and how it is a logical consequence of looking at certain things in a certain way.

Here is a simple example of a setup argument. Note that the argument comes first, and the section ends with the question:

- Students struggle with math word problems.
- Relieving students of computational tasks might help them concentrate more fully on the logic and structure of the word problems.
- Therefore, it makes sense to ask the following research question—Do calculators help students do math word problems?

The Support Argument

The *support argument* is the second most common form of research argument. Researchers most often use this type of argument when they feel that the research question per se should make sense to the reader, but nonetheless it still needs to have its case developed. Here is an example, using our basic research question:

- Do calculators help students do math word problems?
- Teachers report that students tend to do better with math word problems when they can use calculators, but this has never been tested scientifically.
- Therefore, this study will take a controlled look at the research question to see if the teachers' observations hold up under scientific scrutiny.

The Setup and Support Argument

This is the least common form of research argument. We find this argument type when the researchers feel they need to first put the research question into some kind of context, and then support the question. Here is an example, using our basic research question:

- Most math students struggle with word problems. In particular, they report that there are too many things to keep straight in doing word problems.
- Do calculators help students do math word problems?
- Calculators may take some of the computational burden off students, making the process simpler and less cumbersome.

In summary, how do you decide what sort of argument is being used in an article? The process is simple:

- Find the research question(s)
- If the article starts with the research question, then it is using a support argument
- If the introductory part of the article ends with the research question, then it is using a setup argument

- If the research question(s) comes somewhere in the middle, then it is using a setup and support argument

Conclusions

In many ways, finding research questions and arguments should be one of the easiest tasks of the research critic. This does not mean, however, that these questions and arguments will always be easy to follow and understand. Nonetheless, the easier it is to find them, the easier it will be to devote our concentration to what the questions and arguments say (and not to how they say it).

The final piece that grounds the Introduction of an article is the documentation of the research and theory that supported the work. As we have said over and over, educational research is a collective activity. That is why it is so important to make one's debts to the research community clear. This is why we will leapfrog the remaining content of the articles, for now, and go straight to the References section.

Chapter Seven

Understanding References

So FAR WE HAVE been following the article as it unfolds, from title to Argument. But now, we will jump to the end and look at what *references* can tell us. The reason for this is simple—even though they physically come at the end (when we use most article formats), references most often refer to material that is covered by the questions and the argument.

For the sake of simplicity, we are looking at the most common reference format in educational research—APA (American Psychological Association) format. In APA format, a given article or book or some of the work is only referenced if it is explicitly cited in the body of the article (usually, but not always, in the Introduction section).

In APA format, when a work is cited in the body of the article, it is done by referring to the authors of the study by last names, and by the date of publication. For instance, we might see Alpha, Beta, and Gamma (2012) in the body of the article. If we wish to know more about this reference, we need only go to the References section. There, we find more complete references to the various works cited, in alphabetical order.

We should also note that some articles, particularly qualitative articles, might follow MLA (Modern Language

Association) format. MLA formats the references by document use in the paper, most often by using a footnote on the page that the reference appears on.

As research critics, we appreciate having the references available to us either at the end of the article, or, in less common cases, as they are cited. This allows us to explore possible citations further. At the same time, we also realize that references embed a great deal of information that can be enhanced by various rearrangements.

In the remainder of this chapter, we will show you several of the most useful rearrangements you can employ when seeking to gain further understanding from the references of a given article. We realize that these rearrangements can often be labor intensive, and so we do not expect research critics to use them every time they try to "unpack" an article. But it is to our advantage to know how to do these rearrangements, and to know what we might expect to get from them, in those cases where such efforts might be critical to understanding a given article.

Rearranging the References

There are five basic ways to arrange references. Two of those ways are in use, and the other three are available to you to create as needed. We will look at all five reference strategies in turn.

Alphabetical

This is the most common type of arrangement. It is the manner used in articles that follow APA formats. Here is a fictional example, taken from the fictional article we unpack in Appendix B:

Alpha, A. & Foxtrot, F. (2008). Teaching hygiene concepts to preschool children using play. *Journal of Childhood Hygiene, 23,* 211–234.

Alpha, A., Foxtrot, F. & Zulu, Z. (2009). Using the wooden block method to teach hygiene to children. *Hygiene*, 45, 9–37.

Bravo, B. (1998). *How children play*. New York: Kelty Press.

Charlie, C. & Whiskey, W. (2009). Testing listening comprehension in noisy play settings. *Childhood Comprehension Reports*, 2, 87–96.

Delta, D. (2011). *Basics of pediatric nutrition*. London: Royal Thames Culbertson.

Hotel, H., Echo, E. & Whiskey, W. (2011). Testing listening comprehension in multicultural play settings. *Childhood Comprehension Reports*, 4, 113–165.

Victor, V. & Golf, G. (2003). Teaching safety concepts to preschool children using play. *Journal of Childhood Safety*, 23, 211–234.

Whiskey, W., Echo, E. & Charlie, C. (2007). Teaching listening comprehension to preschool children using play. *Journal of Childhood Comprehension*, 23, 211–234.

Whiskey, W., Echo, E., Hotel, H. & Charlie, C. (2013). *Preschool listening comprehension and preschool play*. Boston: Preschool Primer Research Press.

Yankee, Y., Golf, G. & Victor, V. (2011). Safety learning in afterschool settings. *Journal of Afterschool Learning*, 21, 67–122.

Yankee, Y. & Victor, V. (2007). Identifying basic safety concepts for young children using play self-reports. *Journal of Pediatric Self-Report*, 33, 23–45.

Zulu, Z. & Alpha, A. (2012). Expanding hygiene education by play from preschool to kindergarten. *Journal of Basic Kindergarten Research*, 65, 1066–1078.

Usage

This is the second most common type of arrangement. It is the manner used in articles that follow MLA and related formats. References are cited as footnotes on the page they are referenced, or sometimes as endnotes. In educational research articles, this is not a common form of referencing.

Here are the same references, this time listed in the order of citation:

Delta, D. (2011). *Basics of pediatric nutrition*. London: Royal Thames Culbertson.

Alpha, A., Foxtrot, F. & Zulu, Z. (2009). Using the wooden block method to teach hygiene to children. *Hygiene*, 45, 9–37.

Bravo, B. (1998). *How children play*. New York: Kelty Press.

Victor, V. & Golf, G. (2003). Teaching safety concepts to preschool children using play. *Journal of Childhood Safety*, 23, 211–234.

Yankee, Y. & Victor, V. (2007). Identifying basic safety concepts for young children using play self-reports. *Journal of Pediatric Self-Report*, 33, 23–45.

Yankee, Y., Golf, G. & Victor, V. (2011). Safety learning in afterschool settings. *Journal of Afterschool Learning*, 21, 67–122.

Alpha, A. & Foxtrot, F. (2008). Teaching hygiene concepts to preschool children using play. *Journal of Childhood Hygiene*, 23, 211–234.

Zulu, Z. & Alpha, A. (2012). Expanding hygiene education by play from preschool to kindergarten. *Journal of Basic Kindergarten Research*, 65, 1066–1078.

Whiskey, W., Echo, E. & Charlie, C. (2007). Teaching listening comprehension to preschool children using play. *Journal of Childhood Comprehension*, 23, 211–234.

Charlie, C. & Whiskey, W. (2009). Testing listening comprehension in noisy play settings. *Childhood Comprehension Reports*, 2, 87–96.

Hotel, H., Echo, E. & Whiskey, W. (2011). Testing listening comprehension in multicultural play settings. *Childhood Comprehension Reports*, 4, 113–165.

Whiskey, W., Echo, E., Hotel, H. & Charlie, C. (2013). *Preschool listening comprehension and preschool play*. Boston: Preschool Primer Research Press.

Time

This is an alternative arrangement that you can employ to help you understand how the researchers have tapped into articles across some span of time. Are they looking at work over a broader or narrower range of time? Are the articles older or newer? What is the rough ratio of older to newer work cited? These are some of the questions that can be answered by rearranging the references on a time dimension.

Here is the same set of references, this time organized from oldest to newest:

Bravo, B. (1998). *How children play.* New York: Kelty Press.

Victor, V. & Golf, G. (2003). Teaching safety concepts to preschool children using play. *Journal of Childhood Safety,* 23, 211–234.

Whiskey, W., Echo, E. & Charlie, C. (2007). Teaching listening comprehension to preschool children using play. *Journal of Childhood Comprehension,* 23, 211–234.

Yankee, Y. & Victor, V. (2007). Identifying basic safety concepts for young children using play self-reports. *Journal of Pediatric Self-Report,* 33, 23–45.

Alpha, A. & Foxtrot, F. (2008). Teaching hygiene concepts to preschool children using play. *Journal of Childhood Hygiene,* 23, 211–234.

Alpha, A., Foxtrot, F. & Zulu, Z. (2009). Using the wooden block method to teach hygiene to children. *Hygiene,* 45, 9–37.

Charlie, C. & Whiskey, W. (2009). Testing listening comprehension in noisy play settings. *Childhood Comprehension Reports,* 2, 87–96.

Delta, D. (2011). *Basics of pediatric nutrition.* London: Royal Thames Culbertson.

Hotel, H., Echo, E. & Whiskey, W. (2011). Testing listening comprehension in multicultural play settings. *Childhood Comprehension Reports,* 4, 113–165.

Yankee, Y., Golf, G. & Victor, V. (2011). Safety learning in afterschool settings. *Journal of Afterschool Learning,* 21, 67–122.

Zulu, Z. & Alpha, A. (2012). Expanding hygiene education by play from preschool to kindergarten. *Journal of Basic Kindergarten Research,* 65, 1066–1078.

Whiskey, W., Echo, E., Hotel, H. & Charlie, C. (2013). *Preschool listening comprehension and preschool play.* Boston: Preschool Primer Research Press.

The works cited ranged from 1998 to 2013. However, all but one of them was from 2003 to 2013, which is a ten-year span. Seven of those eleven works were also within a five-year span. So we can conclude that most of the works cited were within the time frame of 2008 to 2013.

Topic

This is an alternative arrangement that you can employ to help you understand the main topics that the references address. By identifying the number of topics, we can get a gauge on those issues the researchers felt were most relevant to the article.

Here is the same set of references, this time organized by topics:

(*This is the Safety and Play topic*)
Victor, V. & Golf, G. (2003). Teaching safety concepts to preschool children using play. *Journal of Childhood Safety*, 23, 211–234.
Yankee, Y. & Victor, V. (2007). Identifying basic safety concepts for young children using play self-reports. *Journal of Pediatric Self-Report*, 33, 23–45.
Yankee, Y., Golf, G. & Victor, V. (2011). Safety learning in afterschool settings. *Journal of Afterschool Learning*, 21, 67–122.
Bravo, B. (1998). *How children play*. New York: Kelty Press.

(*This is the Hygiene and Nutrition topic*)
Alpha, A. & Foxtrot, F. (2008). Teaching hygiene concepts to preschool children using play. *Journal of Childhood Hygiene*, 23, 211–234.
Alpha, A., Foxtrot, F. & Zulu, Z. (2009). Using the wooden block method to teach hygiene to children. *Hygiene*, 45, 9–37.
Zulu, Z. & Alpha, A. (2012). Expanding hygiene education by play from preschool to kindergarten. *Journal of Basic Kindergarten Research*, 65, 1066–1078.
Delta, D. (2011). *Basics of pediatric nutrition*. London: Royal Thames Culbertson.

(*This is the Listening Comprehension topic*)
Whiskey, W., Echo, E. & Charlie, C. (2007). Teaching listening comprehension to preschool children using play. *Journal of Childhood Comprehension*, 23, 211–234.
Charlie, C. & Whiskey, W. (2009). Testing listening comprehension in noisy play settings. *Childhood Comprehension Reports*, 2, 87–96.
Hotel, H., Echo, E. & Whiskey, W. (2011). Testing listening comprehension in multicultural play settings. *Childhood Comprehension Reports*, 4, 113–165.
Whiskey, W., Echo, E., Hotel, H. & Charlie, C. (2013). *Preschool listening comprehension and preschool play*. Boston: Preschool Primer Research Press.

From this rearrangement, we come to find that there are three main topic areas. Furthermore, two of those three topic areas involved research that was not directly relevant to their study but demonstrated the use of their play approach to other areas—namely, safety and listening comprehension.

Team

This is an alternative arrangement that you can employ to help you build "teams" of researchers whose work has influenced this article. When we look at research teams, we get a clearer picture of who is doing relevant work, and how those researchers relate to each other.

Here is the same set of references, this time organized by research teams:

(*This is the Alpha team*)
Alpha, A. & Foxtrot, F. (2008). Teaching hygiene concepts to preschool children using play. *Journal of Childhood Hygiene*, 23, 211–234.
Alpha, A., Foxtrot, F. & Zulu, Z. (2009). Using the wooden block method to teach hygiene to children. *Hygiene*, 45, 9–37.
Zulu, Z. & Alpha, A. (2012). Expanding hygiene education by play from preschool to kindergarten. *Journal of Basic Kindergarten Research*, 65, 1066–1078.

(*This is the Victor team*)
Victor, V. & Golf, G. (2003). Teaching safety concepts to preschool children using play. *Journal of Childhood Safety*, 23, 211–234.
Yankee, Y. & Victor, V. (2007). Identifying basic safety concepts for young children using play self-reports. *Journal of Pediatric Self-Report*, 33, 23–45.
Yankee, Y., Golf, G. & Victor, V. (2011). Safety learning in afterschool settings. *Journal of Afterschool Learning*, 21, 67–122.

(*This is the Whiskey team*)
Whiskey, W., Echo, E. & Charlie, C. (2007). Teaching listening comprehension to preschool children using play. *Journal of Childhood Comprehension*, 23, 211–234.

Charlie, C. & Whiskey, W. (2009). Testing listening comprehension in noisy play settings. *Childhood Comprehension Reports*, 2, 87–96.

Hotel, H., Echo, E. & Whiskey, W. (2011). Testing listening comprehension in multicultural play settings. *Childhood Comprehension Reports*, 4, 113–165.

Whiskey, W., Echo, E., Hotel, H. & Charlie, C. (2013). *Preschool listening comprehension and preschool play*. Boston: Preschool Primer Research Press.

In this case, there were three primary teams. Interestingly enough, these teams also corresponded to the three topic areas. This is not an unusual finding and serves to demonstrate how research teams and topics are often intertwined.

Conclusions

As you can see, arranging and rearranging references can be a great deal of work. When does it make sense to do this? Usually, this strategy works best when there are a great number of references or topics, or both. In this case, by breaking the references down into chunks, it is easier to evaluate the role of these references in the article.

The References section is the last piece of the Introduction materials. By now, you should have a clearer grasp of what the researchers intend to do. The next question is—how are they going to do it? We will address this explicitly when we look at Methods and Procedures.

Chapter Eight

Understanding Methods and Procedures

AFTER THE INTRODUCTION, WE find the Methods (or Procedures) section. In this very important section, we will learn just exactly how the researchers plan to answer their research questions.

The best trick to remember what should be covered in a Methods or Procedures section is the simple journalistic strategy for gathering information. The researchers need to answer the following questions—who, what, when, where, and how.

Who?

Educational research articles, more often than not, look at the actions and behaviors of human beings. Depending on the type of study, those actions and behaviors are observed or manipulated. In an ideal world, researchers would be able to study every single relevant person or group. But nearly all the time, this is logistically impossible. So researchers turn to sampling strategies instead.

Sampling

Just about every research article uses some kind of sample. Sampling strategies and details are the "who" part of the Methods or Procedures section.

Types of Samples

There are a number of sampling strategies that are used in educational research. Here are some of the main sampling types.

Random Sample This is one of the most commonly used strategies. A random sample occurs when the researchers decide to use some, but not all, of the people or items that are available. They decide how many of those people or items they will actually use, and then they randomly select that many from the available pool. Most of the time, researchers will use a random number generator to make sure that the sample has been truly randomly selected.

There are two primary ways that random samples are used:

- To get a random subset from a larger set of people or items. This random subset is then used as a substitute for the larger set.
- To divide people from an available group into two or more random subsets, usually for testing hypotheses. Random selection is used here to make sure the two or more groups are as similar to each other as possible. For instance, a group of people can be randomly assigned into either a treatment or a control group.

Stratified Sample In a stratified sample, a process is used to select a certain number of certain types of items or people. This is done to make sure that the eventual sample shares as many of the important characteristics of the target population as possible. Most of the time, researchers lay out those characteristics they consider important ahead of time, so that they can ensure the presence and proper makeup of those characteristics in their sample. Here are two fictional examples to illustrate some of the uses of stratified samples:

- In an election poll, researchers are careful to make sure the demographics of their sample (e.g., age, gender, income, cell phone usage, and the like) mirror as closely as possible the demographics of the population of likely voters.
- Researchers who are looking at cognitive processing in young children often seek to make sure their sample contains a representative spread of children from different social and income levels, to make sure the research is as realistic as possible.

Purposive Sample This sampling strategy is found most often in qualitative studies. In this case, the sample consists of persons who have unique backgrounds or characteristics that make them the target of closer individual study. For instance, researchers might want to study successful math students from impoverished school districts, or homeless children who have attended three or more different schools in a given year, or musical prodigies.

Secondary Sample This form of sampling is found when researchers tap into large databases that we generated for some kind of earlier research study. Given the large amount of data available, it makes sense for researchers to go back to these data and look for other patterns to discern or hypotheses to test. For example, researchers might choose to look at college admissions test data to see if there are, say, gender or state or age patterns that were not identified in the original analysis of the data. This is one of the rare sampling strategies that involves only data, and not people directly.

Convenience Sample A convenience sample is exactly what it sounds like. It is a sample from the larger population that is conveniently available to the researchers. For instance, researchers might be interested in the performance of all third graders in the United States, but they draw their sample for study from a local elementary school.

The primary reason for convenience sampling is the fact that data collection is often expensive and time consuming, and making use of local resources is often the only realistic way to proceed. While it is normal to feel a bit nervous about convenience sampling, more often than not it turns out that this sort of sampling is perfectly legitimate. Consider those researchers looking at third graders. The likelihood is that the third graders in their neighborhood school are reasonably comparable to third graders anywhere else in the United States, especially if the variables studied have nothing to do with local issues or conditions.

What?

In most research studies, key variables are identified to measure. How are those variables then measured, and how are these measures collected? This is the role of *instrumentation* or *data gathering*. Data gathering and instrumentation questions deal with the "what" part of the Methods or Procedures section.

Instrumentation

In order to answer the research question(s), almost always data will need to be gathered. In the case of instrumentation, those data are gathered using some form of instrument. Here is a representative sample of possible instruments that researchers often use to gather data:

- Checklists, where the frequencies of relevant variables are identified and recorded

- Tests that participants take to measure certain (usually psychological) variables such as anxiety, depression, stress, and the like
- Tests to measure a variable of cognitive abilities, such as comprehension and memory
- Self-report opinion and attitude surveys

Other Modes of Data Gathering

In many studies, instrumentation is often not possible or desirable. In those cases, a variety of other data gathering procedures and strategies can be used. Here is a representative sample of some of those procedures:

- Basic observation, where the researchers observe and document what is happening
- Audio or video taping of participants, either singly or collectively
- Measuring various physical data and responses, including medical samples or reaction times
- Analyzing school projects or test data
- Gathering data from public sources, including the Internet
- Gaining access to private or specialized data sources or collections

How?

In the Introductory sections of research articles, research questions have been raised. Now, how do the researchers plan to answer these questions?

Design and Analysis

Design and *analysis* issues address the "how" part of the Methods or Procedures section. There are myriad ways that studies can be designed and analyzed, so all we can do here is outline the basic logic of these processes and point out some of the key examples.

Design The design is the actual plan for answering the research questions. We have already looked at the general designs for quantitative studies (i.e., organizing, finding relationships, testing hypotheses, and building models) and qualitative studies (discovering meaning, investigating, seeking illumination, and participating). Here we will address some of the major practical issues that often arise when researchers implement designs:

- Researchers have to be careful to identify and properly measure the correct variables they need to answer their research questions. For instance, if they are looking at the impact of test anxiety, they need to make sure they are not measuring generalized anxiety instead.
- Researchers need to isolate relevant variables if they are doing quantitative work. Again, if they are looking at test anxiety, they need to show how they have isolated this variable so that they are looking at it directly. More often than not, this involves careful instrumentation and data gathering.
- Researchers need to control variables that may interfere with their findings if they are doing quantitative work. Ideally, researchers like to remove these variables whenever possible. Some variables, like differences in IQ among their participants, cannot be removed. In those cases, researchers often try to randomize those variables across groups, so that they are not systematically over-loaded in one group and under-loaded in another.
- When doing qualitative work, researchers need to be careful to make sure that their participants are giving them as true and accurate a picture as possible. Usually, this involves collecting data from multiple sources and then

making sure that these multiple sources agree with each other. This process is often called *triangulation*.

- Finally, when doing qualitative work, researchers need to make sure they are getting as complete a picture as possible. To ensure this is the case, they often continue to collect data until the data start to repeat themselves and nothing new shows up. This process is often called *saturation*.

Finally, researchers often build upon general design models to utilize technique-specific designs. Here is a list and brief descriptions of some of the more common technique-specific design types used, in both quantitative and qualitative research.

Correlational Design In a correlational design, two or more variables are compared with each other, to see if there are patterns of relationships among these variables. Often, correlational designs are used as precursors to experimental designs. For instance, in medical research, correlations between smoking and lung cancer were used to support more precise experimental research to determine whether smoking caused lung cancer.

Experimental Design In an experimental design, hypotheses are tested by isolating and controlling relevant variables. If the isolation and control are precise enough, this allows researchers to claim that one or more variables might indeed cause changes in one or more other variables. Because it deals with causation, experimental design is considered to be the most advantageous of all quantitative designs, to be used whenever possible.

Quasi-Experimental Design This is one of the most common designs used in educational research. In a quasi-experimental design, preexisting and often ongoing processes are treated as if they were actual experimental manipulations, and their impacts are then measured. In a famous series of studies, for instance, it was shown that reductions in class sizes significantly improved test scores for students.

Meta-Analysis These are analyses of analyses, so to speak. That is, a meta-analysis gathers the results of a number of similar studies, to determine what results and findings these studies all have in common.

Computer Simulation As computer power continues to increase, so do the instances of using computers to "crunch" vast amounts of data and create simulations of various educational processes.

Grounded Theory Grounded theory is the most "quantitative" looking form of qualitative research. By using careful observation strategies, grounded theorists seek to collect data and observations from the ground up and then build code structures to eventually create theory. This theory is the exact opposite of traditional theory building, where theories are first proposed and then tested.

Analysis Analysis describes the procedures that will be used to test the data generated by the design. Because there are so many different analysis strategies, we will summarize briefly some of the key analytic techniques by design:

- Correlational designs use various forms of correlation coefficients. The most common types are the Pearson product-moment correlation (comparing two variables), multiple correlations (when more than two variables are being compared), Spearman rho correlations (used with ranking data), and point-biserial correlations (used with categorical data).
- Experimental and quasi-experimental designs that test hypotheses use the same analytic tools. Some of the most

common tools are the independent-t (where two groups are compared), dependent-t (where measures from the same group at two different times or conditions are compared), and ANOVA ([ANalysis Of VAriance], where more than two groups or conditions are compared—there are a vast number of ANOVA designs for all sorts of differing testing conditions, so pay attention to exactly what the researchers are trying to test here).

- Simple modeling designs use multiple regression techniques. Multiple regression in essence seeks to improve the predictability of a target variable by considering its relation to relevant other variables. As modeling strategies grow more complex, they use such techniques as logistic regression, cohort analysis, and structural equation modeling, among others. High-level computer simulations use procedures like Monte Carlo techniques. Describing how all these models work is beyond our scope here.

Special Logistical Concerns

Most of the time, research studies try to be as generalizable as possible. Under certain conditions, some characteristics of the research setting actually play an important role. If those characteristics involve issues of time, then they address the "when" part of the Methods or Procedures section. If those characteristics are tied to the specific setting of the research, then they address the "where" aspects of the Methods or Procedures.

When?

Time can play a key role in certain types of research studies. The most important role time can play is when it is built into the design of the study. In fact, there are three primary uses of time that we find in some educational research designs:

- In a repeated measures design, the sample is measured on more than two occasions on some target variable (say, memory for numbers). All participants in a group are subjected to all treatments, each group serving as its own control. Variations of the design include the factorial repeated measure and the counterbalanced repeated measures design.
- In a straightforward pre-post design, a group of participants is measured on a key variable both before and after some kind of intervention. These two sets of scores are then compared on a case-by-case basis to see if there has been some change as a result of the intervention.
- In a repeated measures design, the sample is divided into a treatment group and a control group. Each group is measured initially on some target variable (say, memory for numbers). At the outset, there should be no difference between these groups, since they should be equivalent samples. After the treatment, the two groups are remeasured. If the treatment is effective, then the groups should differ in their performance, with the treatment group outperforming the control group.
- Longitudinal designs involve measuring targeted variables over time. A longitudinal study measures some key set of variables at the outset for a given group, and that group is followed (and systematically remeasured) over the years. Studies of groups of twins are a well-known example of longitudinal research.
- Sometimes, we can see a cohort effect in a study. A cohort effect occurs when a particular era is targeted for special study. In some cases, this cohort effect is seen as a confounding variable for various longitudinal studies. However, at times the cohort itself is so interesting that it merits further study on its own terms. For instance, the impact of the baby boomers on the educational system in the United States has been the target of considerable research over the years.

Where?

In most research studies, the role of the physical location of the study is intentionally minimized. This is due primarily to the desire of the researchers to make their research as generalizable as possible. One key way to ensure this is to look at things that could be looked at in any number of settings. For instance, learning fractions should be a similar experience in both Tulsa and Timbuktu. Therefore, in most quantitative studies, there are no major locale issues.

Location factors, however, can often play a role in qualitative studies. In ethnographies, for instance, the location of the research can play a key role. Special locations, such as successful classrooms in failing schools and school districts, are an example of these sorts of targets for closer examination.

Conclusions

Methods or Procedures sections not only lay out the key logistical parameters of a study, but they also serve as a blueprint for future researchers who might either replicate or extend the study in question. Either way, a clear Methods or Procedures section grounds the theoretical aspects of the research into real world parameters. If done right, Methods or Procedures sections clear the way for the reader to pay attention to the findings, without worrying about where they came from or how they were gathered.

In the next two chapters, we will look at Results and Findings directly. We will start with Quantitative Results and Findings, and then move on to Qualitative Results and Findings.

Chapter Nine

Understanding Quantitative Results and Findings

EVERY RESEARCH STUDY PRESENTS *results* (or *findings*). Ideally, these results are the answers to the research questions raised earlier. In this chapter, we will look at some of the kinds of results we might expect to find in quantitative research articles.

As we have said over and over again, the goal of a research study is to answer its research questions. There are essentially four types of research questions that are asked in quantitative studies:

- Are the characteristics of the various samples, groups, and/or subgroups in terms of the key variables that are measured in this study representative of the target population? And what tools can we use to organize and describe our data so that we can make systematic decisions about their characteristics?
- What are the various relationships among key variables that are measured in this study, and what tools can we use to see if these relationships are significant or not?

- What tools can we use to test the hypotheses that are raised within this study, to see if they are significant or not?
- What tools can we use to organize various relationships among key variables into models to explain and/or predict target behaviors or objectives, and to determine if these models are significantly effective?

Tools for Organizing and Describing

One of the most important research questions for any given study is often assumed and not stated explicitly. But at the same time it is usually answered before any other questions are tackled. These research questions deal with clarifying the characteristics of the study. Clarifications can deal with either the sample or the data, or most often with both.

Sample Characteristics

Researchers often need to answer the following question: Is there a good match between the sample used and the population that is being studied?

In rare cases, sampling is not an issue, because the entire population is being studied all at once. However, most educational research studies target big populations, like all third graders in the United States or all elementary teachers or the like. In those cases, the researchers have to sample.

When looking at sample characteristics, researchers need to address two main issues: are the sample characteristics similar to the population characteristics, and, when there are groups and/or subgroups involved, are all of those groups and subgroups similar enough to each other in terms of their basic demographics?

In the case of sample to population comparisons, it is very helpful when the demographics of the population itself are known. For instance, we know that any large group of people will have a mean IQ around one hundred. Therefore, if we are looking for a sample of the population as a whole, we would be concerned if our sample had an average IQ that was much larger or much smaller than one hundred.

In the case of group-to-group comparisons, the process is much simpler and more straightforward. The researchers simply measure the basic demographics of each group and compare those measures to each other. If they are reasonably close to being the same, then it is reasonable to assume that these groups are samples from the same general population.

Data Characteristics

We need to remember that *data* is a plural noun. Each individual person or thing contributes a single measure, or a *datum*. Therefore, when we talk of data, we are talking about a collective measure. This is an important point, since most of the time in quantitative research we are interested in group behaviors and/or performances, and not what any one individual might do. That is why we treat our groups as distributions.

In our discussion of statistical literacy, we talked about how collected measures from a group form a distribution. A distribution is a set of measurements of a single variable for a given sample or population. Every distribution has two indices that tell us two crucial things—what our typical scores are for that distribution and the range of variability for those scores. The first score type deals with central tendency and the second deals with dispersion. We will look at each in turn.

Central Tendency Central tendency helps us identify those scores that tend to cluster together in some way. There are three common measures of central tendency:

> **Mode** This is the most common value. We only use the mode when we are looking at categories. For instance,

if we are fishing in a freshwater lake, we might be catching bluegill, bass, and catfish. If we catch eleven bluegill, fourteen bass, and twenty-five catfish, then our mode is "catfish." That is, catfish is the most common fish we caught.

Median This is the middle score of a collection of scores. That is, it is the fiftieth percentile score, or the score value that divides the distribution into two equal halves. For instance, we might say that the median income in Researchlandia is $25,000. If there are 100,000 people in Researchlandia who earn an income, then half of them earn $25,000 or less and half of them earn more than $25,000.

Mean The mean is the average score in a collection of scores. You get the mean by adding together all the scores and then dividing by the number of scores. The mean is much more precise than the mode or median because it takes into account each and every score in creating this average. The only time the median is better is when there are a number of either very high or very low scores. In a symmetric set of scores, the mean, median, and mode will be the same. Another important aspect of the mean is the fact that, in the absence of any further information, the mean is the best single prediction of any single score. Prediction models use this fact by starting with the mean and then adding additional information to predict scores.

Dispersion Almost all the time, we will not get the same scores for everyone in a distribution. For one thing, we are measuring variables, so we expect some variability. But how can we determine how these scores disperse from some central cluster in a meaningful way? This measure is what we call dispersion, and there are two common measures of dispersion:

Range Modes and medians (and means as well) are measures of the most common or typical scores. But when we are looking at a collection of scores, we need to know more than just the common or typical scores. We need to know the range of scores. If the range is very narrow, then we know that any one score is not all that different from the typical score. But if the range is wide, then we know that there is a lot of variation, and that any one score may or may not look like a typical score. This information is important when we try to interpret our collective scores. For example, when we look at the incomes in Researchlandia, a range of incomes from $20,000 to $30,000 tells us that incomes are fairly uniform, while a range from $5,000 to $300,000 is describing a much different and more diverse situation.

Standard Deviation The standard deviation is a type of range that, like the mean, takes into consideration the values of each and every score. This allows us to say some very precise things about the ways that our scores vary. In a deeper mathematical sense, the standard deviation is also a measure of points of inflections. A point of inflection is a place where the nature of the patterning of the scores changes. For instance, the scores within one standard deviation above and one standard deviation below the mean are, for all intents and purposes, pretty much the same as the mean. Those outside this range should be considered to be different from the mean.

All of these descriptive measures work together to give the reader a picture of the distributions that occur within a study.

* * *

At this point, we are ready to look at the remaining three types of questions that are often asked, and the tools that researchers use to get the results they are looking for.

Tools for Finding and Evaluating Relationships

Some research questions are built around finding and evaluating the relationships among two or more variables. There are two kinds of potential relationships among variables—naturally occurring relationships and relationships that researchers create or manipulate. When relationships are created or manipulated, they are almost always done for the sake of testing hypotheses. Therefore, these sorts of relationships will be examined a bit later when we look at tools for testing hypotheses. In this section, we will focus instead on tools used to look at and evaluate relationships that are more or less natural in nature. To this end, we will look at two key types of relationships that are common in educational research.

Frequency Patterns In this situation, researchers are looking at common frequency patterns among two or more naturally occurring variables. These patterns can either show the reader a picture of how these frequencies coexist or interact, or else they can be tested by the researchers to see if these patterns are what we might naturally expect or not. If they are not what we might expect, this can lead to taking a closer look to see what actually might be happening here.

Most of the time, frequency data will be presented in a table, with a variable on each axis and frequencies reported in the cells of the table. Researchers can then perform a Chi-square analysis, to see whether the actual observed frequencies are in line with what might reasonably be expected.

Consider the following fictional example. A group of one hundred single people with pets are selected. There are fifty men and fifty women. Some of them have dogs and some have cats. It might be reasonable to expect that twenty-five of the men have dogs and twenty-five of them have cats, with the same kind of pattern of dogs and cats for the women. When we gather our data (which are usually put into a table for ease of reading), we find the dog:cat ratio for men is 15:35 and the dog:cat ratio for women is 42:8.

These results look different from what we might have expected, but sometimes looks can be deceiving. By performing a Chi-square analysis, we can determine how likely it is that our observed frequencies are different from our expected frequencies. To do this, the researchers perform a significance test. In the case of Chi-square, the actual Chi-square is compared to a critical value. The critical value is the value Chi-square would have to be equal to or be less than for the test to be nonsignificant. As always, the level of significance is chosen beforehand, and usually is either p<.05 or p<.01.

If the Chi-square is significant, then we can say with some degree of likelihood that our two types of frequencies are different from each other, and most probably represent different possible situations.

We also need to note that Chi-square analyses use degrees of freedom. In this case, though, the degrees of freedom are not based on sample sizes but on the number of cells in the frequency chart. So, for instance, if the chart looks at three levels of frequencies, the degree of freedom for the Chi-square analysis is equal to two.

Correlational Relationships Correlational analysis is one of the major tools in educational research. When researchers use correlations, they are looking to see if two (or sometimes more) variables change systematically in relation to each other. That change can be either direct (both variables go up or down at the same time) or inverse (when one variable goes up the other goes down, and vice versa).

The most common form of correlation coefficient (which is used to compare two variables to each other) is the Pearson product-moment correlation, or r_{xy}. The x and y indicate the two variables, and the r stands for relationship. The Pearson product-moment correlation is actually an index, so its values range from +1 to -1. The closer the value of r is to +1, the closer it is to being a perfect direct relationship. The closer it is to -1, the closer it is to being a perfect inverse relationship. When the value of r is close to zero, then there is no relationship between the two variables.

In a manner similar to the significance test of the Chi-square analysis, a critical level of significance is chosen beforehand. If the actual r-value is higher than the critical value (again usually at the p<.05 or p<.01 level), then the correlation is significantly greater than zero. If the r-value is positive and significant, then there is a significant direct relationship. If the r-value is negative and significant, then there is a significant inverse relationship.

Sample sizes matter for correlations, so degrees of freedom must be reported and used. In this case, the degrees of freedom are based on the number of pairs of measurements taken on both variables.

One final point needs to be kept in mind. Correlations only measure relationships. They do not say anything about why those relationships exist, or whether one variable caused the other. To move to this next higher step, researchers need to create and test hypotheses.

Tools for Testing Hypotheses

Many research questions are often formulated as hypotheses, and the test of these hypotheses is the basis for answering these research questions. This is because testing hypotheses is a stronger action than finding relationships, and as such can be used to support claims that one or more variables might cause changes in the dependent variable. There are two basic and primary tools used to test hypotheses:

t-tests The simplest tool to test hypotheses is the t-test. In essence, the t-test is a way to compare means. There are two basic forms of the t-test: the independent t-test and the dependent t-test.

The independent t-test is sometimes called the grouped t-test, because it is used to compare two groups. Most often, the groups are a treatment group and a control group. The scores for each group are collected and put into a distribution, so that each group has its own mean and standard deviation. Then, the means for each group are adjusted to take into account any differences in sample sizes and any differences in dispersion. These adjusted means are then compared to each other. If there are no differences between the groups, then the t-value will be zero. As with other tests of significance, a critical value is computed for the t-test at either $p<.05$ or $p<.01$. If the actual value of the t-test exceeds this critical value, then the finding is significant and there is most likely a real difference in the treatment group scores and the control group scores. Degrees of freedom are used to help determine critical values, and they are based on the number of scores in each group.

The dependent t-test is sometimes called the paired t-test, since it uses scores from the same participants collected at different times or under different conditions. The differences between these two scores are computed, and these differences then form a distribution with its own mean and standard deviation. If this mean of difference scores is zero, then there are no differences between the two measuring conditions. As we have seen before, it is necessary to determine a critical value ahead of time for this difference score at either the $p<.05$ or the $p<.01$ level. If the actual difference score exceeds this critical value, then the difference is significant. Degrees of freedom are also used to help determine critical values, and they are based on the number of difference scores. The dependent t-test is sometimes called the paired t-test, since it uses scores from the same participants collected at different times or under different conditions or matched pairs and dyads (e.g., twins, brother and sister).

ANOVA ANOVA stands for ANalysis Of VAriance. ANOVA designs are used when there are more than two levels of variables involved. ANOVA designs can be simple, where three or more levels of a single independent variable are compared, to complex factorial and nested designs, where various levels of the design interact with each other. The complexity of any given ANOVA design should be based on the research questions being tested—the design should be just complex enough (and no more) to address the research questions it was designed to test.

Where the t-test works with means, ANOVA works with the amount of variance that is available. Variance is a measure of the overall change that was found. That variance comes from two, and only two, sources. There is *within* variance, which is the natural variance that we might expect among any group of scores within a given group. Then there is *between* variance, which is the variance found between the various groups. These two sources add up to form the *total* variance. Because these two groups can be added together to form the total, they are independent of each other.

When the between variance (adjusted for the number of groups) is divided by the within variance (adjusted for the number of scores within each given group), then we get what is called the F ratio. If this ratio is less than one, this means that most of the variance in this study is due to natural variation within its groups, and therefore there can be no significant findings. The larger the F ratio, the more likely the variance between the groups is significant.

As with a number of other inferential methods, there is a critical value for each particular case. This critical value is usually set at the p<.05 or p<.01 level. And as before, if the F ratio exceeds this critical value, then the differences between the groups is significant.

Degrees of freedom are computed for both the between variance and the within variance, and are used collectively to set the appropriate critical level. No matter how complicated the ANOVA design ends up being, in the end all the degrees of freedom must add up to the total degrees of freedom of the total sample. This is one way to check to see if researchers are indeed on track with the mechanics of their analyses.

Tools for Building and Evaluating Models

Over the past few decades, the number of modeling tools has proliferated in educational research. For that reason, it is impossible to cover all of them. Instead, we will concentrate on the first and simplest type of model in quantitative research—regression analysis.

Regression Analysis

When we are trying to predict the value for a single individual within a group, the best place to start from is the mean. That is, in the absence of any further information, the mean is the single best predictor. For instance, suppose you are given one single third grader in a classroom somewhere, and you are asked to predict her IQ. In the absence of any other information, your best guess is one hundred, since that is the population average.

How can you improve that prediction? This is where regression techniques come in. You can use regression to look at the impact of another relevant variable.

For instance, let's go back to our third grader. Suppose we find out that she tests in the ninety-ninth percentile for cognitive ability. This additional piece of information suggests that it would be reasonable to assume that her IQ is higher than one hundred. But this assumption needs to be tested.

In a regression analysis design, the mean is replaced with an equation that takes into account the correlation between the reading comprehension test and IQ. This will be a straight-line equation. Like all straight-line equations, this equation will have a constant slope, which in this case is called the standardized, or beta, slope. If this slope is greater than zero (which is tested by using a simple t-test), then it says that this equation is a better predictor of any given individual score than the mean would be.

Finally, the regression equation needs to show that it can account for a significant amount of variation in the overall scores. That is, just how much of the overall variation is being addressed by the equation? This leads to a form of correlation measure called the R^2. This measure is evaluated using an F-test (ANOVA) with an appropriate critical value to see if there is a significant improvement in the amount of overall variance that is accounted for by the equation. That F-test will have one degree of freedom for the between variation (for the comparison) and the appropriate number of degrees of freedom based on the overall sample size.

Presentation of Results

So far, we have looked at the tools that researchers use to present their results, at least in a very general and global way. But in most studies, researchers assume that their audience is already acquainted to some degree with the nature and use of these tools, and so what researchers tend to do is to just mention and use them. Therefore, the preceding discussion of tools was meant to familiarize you, as an emerging research critic, rather than to indicate that there will be a discussion of tools per se in the article. Now we are ready to look at how the results are presented.

In most Results sections, researchers try to present their results as simply and clearly as possible. Most of the time, those findings are presented without further discussion— discussion and conclusions come later, in the Discussion and Conclusions section.

In the meantime, there are certain procedures that researchers most often use to present their findings. Here are some examples from some of the more common types of quantitative results.

Presenting Descriptive Results

Most quantitative studies report descriptive results. These results should give the reader a clear and unambiguous picture of the distributions of the key variables of the sample. These can include

- Percentage data of key demographic variables, such as gender, grade level, and the like
- Means and standard deviations of all key independent and dependent variables
- Any information that is relevant to deciding whether the sample is properly representative of its larger population. Since most variables are normally distributed, this is often a measure of whether all the variables are normally distributed as well.

Presenting Frequency–Based Results

When providing frequency-based results, the researchers should address the following:

- Are the data clearly organized, preferably in tables that are easy to read?
- Are the data presented in an unambiguous fashion, so that any further discussion of them is easy to follow?
- If a Chi-square analysis has been performed, is the value for the Chi-square test clearly labeled and easy to find?
- If a Chi-square analysis has been performed, have the researchers reported whether the results are significant, and to what level of probability?

Here is a typical Chi-square result:

$$\text{Chi-square (df=2, N = 50)} = 17.54^* \quad ^*p<.05$$

What this means is that when the Chi-square analysis was performed, using two degrees of freedom and a sample size of sixty, the score exceeded the critical value at a level greater than 20 to 1, and so it is highly unlikely that the differences between observed and expected frequencies are due solely to chance. Therefore, it is reasonable to assume that our observed frequencies are significantly different, in some way, from our expected frequencies.

Presenting Correlational Results

When providing correlational results, the researchers should address the following:

- Are all variables clearly identified and labeled?
- Do the researchers indicate whether there is a direct or an inverse relationship? Note that if there is no sign, then it is assumed to be a direct relationship.
- If there is more than one correlation being reported, are they presented in a table for easy reading and interpretation?
- Have the researchers indicated both the correct number of degrees of freedom (in this case, N-2) and the level of probability used to select the critical value?

Here is a typical correlation result:

$$r(df=24) = -0.78* \quad *p<.05$$

What this means is that when the correlation was performed, using twenty-four degrees of freedom, then the results indicated an inverse relationship that exceeded the critical value at a level greater than 20 to 1, and so it is highly unlikely that the relationship between these two variables is zero. Therefore, it is reasonable to assume that there is some degree of inverse relationship between the two variables.

Presenting t-Test Results

When providing t-test results (either independent t-test or dependent t-test), the researchers should address the following:

- Are all variables clearly identified?
- For an independent t-test, are the mean and standard deviations of the difference reported?
- For a dependent t-test, are the mean and standard deviation of the difference score reported?
- For either type of t-test, are the degrees of freedom and the probability level reported?

Here is a typical independent t-test result:

Results indicate that students do better on written math quizzes (M = 3.45, SD = 1.11) than with oral math quizzes (M = 3.00, SD = 0.80) t(df=16) = 4.00*   *p<.01

What this means is that two groups of nine students each were given either a written or an oral math quiz. The written group's mean performance was 3.45 right answers, with a standard deviation of 1.1. The oral group's mean performance was 3.00 right answers with a standard deviation of 0.80. When compared to the critical value for a probability level of 100 to 1 when there are sixteen total degrees of freedom, the resulting t-score was significantly different from zero, leading us to conclude that the written group performed better than the oral group.

Here is a typical dependent t-test result:

The twenty-five students had an average difference from pre-test to post-test math ability scores of +4.8 (SD = 5.5); t(df=24) = +4.36*   *p<.05

What this means is that post-test scores after test preparation increased by an average of 4.8 points, which was significant as measured by a dependent t-test with twenty-four degrees of freedom at the 20 to 1 level of probability.

Presenting ANOVA Results

When providing ANOVA results, the researchers should address the following:

- Are all relevant variables properly identified?
- Are the data presented in an unambiguous fashion, so that any further discussion of them is easy to follow?
- Is the total number of participants for each group, and the overall total of participants, properly reported?
- Are the means and standard deviations for each group in the study reported?
- Are the F ratio, with its appropriate between groups and within groups, degrees of freedom clearly reported, along with whether it is significant at the selected level of probability?

Here is a typical ANOVA result:

Out of the total twenty-seven third graders in this study, the twelve participants in the online review group had an average quiz score of 12.3 correct responses (SD = 4.1); the nine participants in the face-to-face review group had an average quiz score of 7.4 correct responses (SD = 2.3); and the eight participants in the control group had an average quiz score of 6.6 correct responses (SD = 3.1). The type of review condition for the quiz, therefore, was significant, $F(2,26) = 8.76*$ *p<.05

What this means is that when the students were divided into three similar (albeit unequal-sized) groups (i.e., online review, face-to-face review, and control), there was an overall significant difference among these groups, as measured by an F-test, at a 20 to 1 level of probability.

Presenting Regression Analysis Results

When providing multiple regression results, the researchers should address the following:

- Are all relevant variables properly identified?
- Are the correlations used to form the regression equation presented in a table for easy reading, interpretation, and identification?
- Is the standardized slope, or beta, reported, and is the t-test of significance of that slope also reported?
- Is the R^2 score reported, along with its F-test score?

Here is a typical multiple regression result:

Reading comprehension scores significantly predicted IQ scores, b = +.34, t(225) = 6.53, p<.01. Reading comprehension scores also explained a significant proportion of variance in IQ scores, R_2 = .12, F(1, 225) = 42.64, p<.01.

What this means is that using the reading comprehension scores allowed the researchers to improve their IQ predictions somewhat, since there was a moderate direct relationship between high reading comprehension scores and high IQs, and lower reading comprehension scores and lower IQs. Furthermore, this variation in reading comprehension scores accounted for about 12 percent of the variation among IQ scores, which was shown to be a modest but significant impact. At the end of the day, however, 88 percent of the variation among IQ scores remained unaccounted for.

From Univariate to Multivariate Results

Before we leave the topic of quantitative results, we need to say a word about multivariate analyses and their results. This is a mode of analysis that was once considered to be too complex to undergo, but the advent of fast computer-based analysis strategies has led to a growing use of these methods.

Conceptually, the notion of multivariate analysis is not that complex. In all of the examples we have used so far, we have looked at only one dependent variable. Such analyses are called univariate (or one variable) analyses.

Multivariate analyses are analyses that replace either the dependent or the independent variable (or both) with a set of related variables. In the case of multiple independent variables, a related set of predictor variables is used. In the case of multiple dependent variables, a single dependent variable is replaced with a matrix of related dependent variables.

Each multivariate analysis has its own set of rules and terms, and looking at them here is beyond the scope of this work. You should remember, though, that conceptually they are not all that different from the analyses and results you have already seen.

Here to help you is a short and incomplete list of comparisons of univariate and multivariate analyses:

- t-test : multivariate t-test
- ANalysis Of VAriance (ANOVA) : Multivariate ANalysis Of VAriance (MANOVA)
- regression analysis : multiple regression, structural equation modeling (SEM)

Conclusions

In the next chapter, we move along to consider Qualitative Results and Findings.

Chapter Ten

Understanding Qualitative
Results and Findings

As we stated earlier, every research study presents results. In this chapter, we will look at the kinds of results we might expect to find in qualitative research articles.

Overall, there are four basic qualitative designs— discovering meaning, investigating, seeking illumination, and participating to right some imbalance or social wrong. All of these designs are linked to research questions in some way, and all of them seek to answer or clarify those questions. It is in this context that we can talk about qualitative research results and findings.

At the outset, we need to make clear that, in at least some qualitative studies, the separation of results and discussions is not clear cut. This is because, especially when dealing with issues of meaning, the discussion of the nature and implications of meaning is often an integral part of the research and its findings.

When we talked about quantitative results and findings, we looked at tools and presentation strategies, in that order. In the case of qualitative results and findings, it is more useful to talk about *orientations* and *strategies* for presenting these results and findings.

There are two major orientations toward results and findings in qualitative research—*thematic analysis* and *meaning discernment*. Cutting across these two orientations are three primary strategies—*sorting and organizing, reflecting and synthesizing,* and *narrating.*

We will look at each of these areas in turn.

Orientations

All forms of qualitative research collect and analyze data. Once those data have been collected, researchers need to make one of three decisions about how to treat those data when they analyze them:

- break into clusters based on themes
- "mine" for valuable and often hidden meaning
- use some combination of these two approaches

Because it is so clear in practice to see when researchers are combining these two orientations, we will focus only on those cases where one or the other orientation is being taken exclusively.

Thematic Analysis

Thematic analysis is based on the assumption that all pieces of qualitative data are inherently organized by larger and more abstract (and sometimes hierarchical) themes. Qualitative analysis then becomes the discovery and testing of these themes, which are then presented with corroborating support and evidence. By working with themes, it becomes easier to tackle and apply complex concepts and situations.

The act of breaking down a complex whole into a set of simpler explanatory themes is one of the primary goals of qualitative research. Therefore, we should expect to find any number of approaches and techniques within thematic analysis, and in fact we do.

Here we will look at examples of three of the myriad types of thematic analyses that are found in qualitative research—grounded theory, focus group analysis, and material analysis. These three examples were chosen to illustrate to some degree the wide range of approaches that are available to researchers.

Grounded Theory Grounded theory is the oldest and most established type of thematic analysis. It depends upon the careful bottom-up coding of data to create working codes (called open codes), more refined and broader codes (usually called axial codes), and eventually a smaller number of final inclusive code areas called themes.

Here is a fictional example of how grounded theory results might be presented:

> Ten students from Mr. Smith's Advanced Placement class were interviewed and their transcripts were analyzed using open coding to generate an eventual set of stable axial categories that served as the basis for generating the themes that were themselves the basis of our eventual theory. This in-depth analysis yielded thirty-three open categories with twelve axial categories that were eventually translated into four broad themes. These themes were Individualized attention; Extensive use of real world examples; Extensive use of visual aids and graphs; and Use of humor.

Focus Group Analysis Focus groups, unlike grounded theory and other similar methodologies, deliberately gather data in a collective manner, so as to see how various participants build and reflect and modify what each other says. In this way, a more interactional picture of what participants believe and act upon can be built.

Here is a fictional example of how focus group analysis results might be presented:

A number of the mothers expressed serious concerns about the nutritional value of the school lunches that were served to their young children: I try to give my children fresh fruits and vegetables, which is tough to do on my salary, and then I find out that they have pizza three times a week for lunch (Monica). I like pizza too, but not three times a week. School is supposed to help expose my children to new healthy kinds of foods, and help them make better choices (Marian). How can the kids make better choices when the people choosing the food have no background or training in nutrition (Yolanda)?

Material Analysis While grounded theory and focus groups (and related methods) build their data around what people say, material analysis looks at what people own and display. Here is a fictional example of how researchers might perform a thematic material analysis of bumper stickers on cars in a particular parking lot:

When looking at the cars in the concert venue VIP parking lot, 120 of the 211 cars had bumper stickers that were deemed relevant to the concert experience itself. Seventy-two of them displayed the band name (Phish), or its logo (a stylized fish), or both. Thirty of the stickers made environmental comments (e.g., Love Your Mother Nature, Phishheads for Forests, Boogie with a Tree Today) that reflect the environmentally friendly consciousness of the band and many of its following, and the final eighteen were either in-jokes or witty references (e.g., Fluffhead for President, NICU Too, Who is this band Phish, and why are they following me all across the country?).

Meaning Discernment

Meaning discernment is based on the assumption that all qualitative data exist on at least two different levels—what is apparent on the surface and what actually (or possibly) might exist at a deeper level.

Hermeneutic Analysis Hermeneutic analysis is a form of meaning discernment that may involve meaning discovery, meaning making, or both. It is rooted in the ancient tradition of extracting meaning from sacred texts. As the concept evolved and expanded, it was first extended to any sort of text, and then to anything that could be "read," from speech to movies and songs and cultural artifacts.

Hermeneutic analysis in qualitative research tends to focus on rooting out the assumptions and perspectives people operate upon when they are in certain experiences. It is a form of digging deeper or putting together seemingly disparate things to create a more coherent picture of meaning in a given situation.

Here is a fictional account of how a researcher might report hermeneutic findings:

> On the wall beside his desk, Mr. Joyce displayed an old child's quilt, hanging on dowel rods from the ceiling. He told me that his second grade students never ask him about the quilt, but that it had been his own blanket from his childhood. "I display the quilt," he said, "because these children come from tough backgrounds and a tough neighborhood. I can't comfort them directly, because they are too suspicious and any kid I would comfort would get singled out for ridicule. But this quilt, which they have the native cunning not to question, helps do some of that soothing for me."

Phenomenological Analysis Hermeneutics is about what words and things *mean*. Phenomenology is about what things mean *to someone*. That is, a phenomenological analysis details how certain ideas or concepts function as a part of lived experience.

When it was first developed, phenomenology was primarily an introspective method, where the researcher examined his or her own lived experience. That aspect of phenomenology still exists, but today it is primarily a method for researchers to uncover and explore the lived experiences of others. Virtually any sort of experience, from dealing with test anxiety or seeking to gain acceptance by one's peers, to serious life setbacks or dealing with a terminal experience, can be examined phenomenologically.

Here is a fictional account of a set of phenomenological research findings:

> When I first look at a test paper (said Mary), the first thing I see is a big black circle in the middle of the page. When I see this circle, I know that I need to keep my wits about me, or I will start getting a headache. So I close my eyes and rub them vigorously until I see stars. For some reason, this helps. It doesn't matter if I know the test material or not—the black circle comes every time. When I was in grade school, I told my teachers, but they got to the point where they didn't believe me. Now I just do what I need to do and hope for the best.

Portraiture Portraiture is a qualitative method that is used when it is particularly important to gain a deeper insight into one or more of the participants. That is, a major part of meaning discernment is observing and deciphering not just what a person does or says, but who that person really is. Portraiture is also used when researchers study unique individuals, or individuals in unique circumstances.

Here is a brief fictional account of a portrait of a research participant:

> Donald was a short, stocky eighth grader with black eyes and sandy hair. From the sag in his shoulders, it was apparent that his backpack was heavy, full of books to take home to the trailer where he and his mom lived. I asked Donald if his mom would mind me visiting. He said, "my mom doesn't like people to come over and see where we live, after my dad left. But she wants to make sure that my video games don't get me into trouble at school, either." He gave me her phone number and I called and she was willing to talk to me.

Strategies

In a manner somewhat independent of the orientation that researchers might take toward their analysis of qualitative data, there are three broad and basic strategies they might use to present those results and findings:

Sorting and Organizing

Sorting and organizing are an integral part of thematic analysis, but they are also important for meaning discernment.

Here is a fictional example of how a thematic analysis finding might be sorted and organized:

> After the initial interviews, participants were sorted into three groups: (1) those who opposed environmental education because it was considered to be superfluous; (2) those who opposed environmental education because it was seen to threaten business education; and (3) those who opposed environmental education because it was considered to be politically progressive.

Here is a fictional example of how a meaning discernment finding might be sorted and organized:

> Truant teens looked at the school police cruisers as a nuisance, while teens who were dealing drugs in the schools and teens who were actively engaged in gang activities viewed the cruisers as the "chariots of an invading army."

Reflecting and Synthesizing

Reflecting and synthesizing are an integral part of meaning discernment, but they are also important for thematic analysis.

Here is a fictional example of how a meaning discernment finding might be synthesized and reflected upon:

Tommy (not his real name) talked about what he felt when he saw a police cruiser slow down to look at him and several of his gang members: They think they know what they see when they see us—just a bunch of gang bangers. What do they know about where I live and what I have to put up with every day? How would they act if the only people they could trust were fellow gang members? How tough would they be then? How would they have the nerve to judge me?

Here is a fictional example of how a thematic analysis finding might be synthesized and reflected upon:

Environmental education teachers learned to develop different interactional strategies with each of the three opposing groups of parents. For the superfluous camp, they held seminars on the value of environmental education. For the business education advocates, they worked with business education teachers to show how both forms of education were necessary. Finally, to address the political issue, they conducted a town-hall panel meeting where advocates across the entire political spectrum spoke in support of environmental education.

Narrating

Regardless of what researchers' orientations toward qualitative results and findings might be, it is clear that narration often plays a key role in how those results and findings are presented.

While qualitative researchers often strive to adhere to similar levels of precision and rigor that quantitative researchers employ, more often than not they do not have the same prescriptively structured analysis tools that quantitative researchers employ. That is why the use of clear and precise narrative techniques is often employed, so as to help in providing order and structure.

Here is a fictional example of a narratively oriented presentation of qualitative findings:

Amanda (not her real name) paced up and down the long dimly lit hallway. Now and then she paused to look at her heavily bandaged wrists. Over the ordinary institutional sounds that cluttered the hallway, she strained to hear some clue about the whereabouts of her infant—a stray cry, a whimper, even a rustling sound. Nothing.

Conclusions

Results and Findings sections are designed to present results and findings in a clear and unambiguous way. They do not, however, discuss what those results and findings might mean, or where they might lead in terms of future research. That is the work of the Discussion or Conclusions section, which is covered in the next chapter.

Chapter Eleven

Understanding Discussions and Conclusions

IT IS NOT ENOUGH for researchers to merely present their results. They must take the further step of showing us what these results mean, and how to contextualize them properly. This is the role of the Discussion and Conclusions section.

Most Discussion and Conclusions sections attempt to cover four major issues—What happened? What was not expected? What do these results mean? Where do we go from here?

Each of these areas will be addressed in turn.

Summary Statements

Most of the time, Discussion and Conclusions sections jump right in to summarize what happened. These are summary statements. The major findings are presented, and then interpreted in light of the research questions.

Here is a set of fictional summary statements, from differing types of studies:

- The major finding of this study was that taking vitamin C in proper pediatric doses helped a majority of disadvantaged preschool children improve their attendance rates dramatically. This effect diminished as the children came from more affluent families, presumably because of the better overall nutritional levels of these children.
- As expected, extracurricular activities and tutoring were significant predictors of senior year GPA. Number of hours spent doing homework was a weaker predictor, as were measures of depression and test anxiety (as negative predictors). Surprisingly, parental involvement and teacher perceptions played little or no roles.
- The demographics of school shooters over the past twenty-five years are extraordinarily consistent. All of them were white males between the ages of fifteen and seventeen, from middle-class and upper-middle-class families. None of them had steady girlfriends and over half of them were failing at least one subject. Fully 90 percent of them had been targeted for disciplinary action by more than one teacher, but in all cases there were no follow-up actions by the schools after the initial disciplinary acts.

Explanation Statements

Usually after there is a summary of results and findings, researchers often engage in explanations. Here we usually find two sorts of explanations. First of all, the researchers often show how the findings match their expectations and hypothesis. Sometimes, the researchers need to explain why some of the results turned out the way they did. We can see both types of explanations in the following fictional examples, which extend the earlier summary statements:

- We hypothesized that one primary reason for decreased attendance among poor preschoolers was the possibility that they get sick more often. One way to improve their attendance is to improve their overall health, particularly in terms of their immune systems. Since vitamin C is a powerful immune system supporter, we are not surprised that its increase was matched by a subsequent increase in attendance for these children. Furthermore, since middle-class children probably have higher nutrition standards and consequently better immune system health, they did not need the boost of the extra vitamin C.

- The fact that parental involvement and teacher perceptions played virtually no role in senior level GPAs requires further examination. We suspect that this is due to the fact that seniors have already made their college and other career choices, and so they are focusing on other issues in preparation for their new lives. Therefore, they seek guidance from parents and teachers not so much on keeping up their grades (which many of them feel they no longer need) and toward other career, education, and life issues.

- A common theme that seems to run through most of these school shooter cases is the relative social and cultural isolation of these young men. While they do not seem to be in need of any material benefits, most of them seem to suffer from a poverty of meaningful human relationships, from families, girlfriends, and social networks in schools. It comes as no surprise that many of them acted out in some way to draw disciplinary attention to themselves, but that attention soon faded away.

Implications Statements

One of the most important things that researchers can do is to reflect upon the potential impact of their research studies. Particularly in an area like educational research, their findings can often have important theoretical and practical implications. Also, this is where researchers need to acknowledge any limitations in their work, and how these limitations might affect the ways that we interpret the findings.

Staying with our three fictional examples, here are some potential implications of that work:

- One of the most exciting implications from this study is the fact that academic preparation and achievement for at-risk preschoolers might be significantly enhanced by improving their nutritional conditions. Given the great deal of knowledge and information about nutrition that are currently available, these sorts of interventions could be implemented almost immediately.
- While these findings shed some interesting light on those factors that influence grades among high school seniors, it is important to acknowledge a number of serious limitations in this study. First of all, we used a relatively small sample size of five high schools within a ten-mile radius of each other. Secondly, these students were overwhelmingly middle- and upper-middle-class students, from relatively homogeneous racial and ethnic backgrounds. Finally, we did not collect any data from the students that might shed light on why certain factors did or did not influence their grades.
- In our research, we were able to identify some common threads among school shooters. Our hope is to improve our chances of identifying young men in the future who might potentially engage in these sorts of terrible acts, so that we can intervene for their sakes and the sake of society in general. The more we understand, the better we will be able to do this.

Expansion Statements

Finally, it is important for researchers to acknowledge how they, or others, can build upon this work in the future.

Again, here are some expansion statements for our three fictional examples:

- Our research on the positive impact of vitamin C on at-risk preschoolers barely scratches the surface. Given the fact that the effects of nutrition are often subtle and nuanced, it is critical that more sophisticated and tightly controlled studies be performed in this area. While it is encouraging to see positive results from this simple study, we cannot delude ourselves into thinking that the path ahead will always be so simple. We need to respect the complexity of both human learning and human biology, but in doing so we can also set ourselves on the path for meaningful research for decades to come.

- While this work represents a good start on gaining further insights on GPA performance for seniors, there are a number of future directions for research that can be immediately beneficial. First of all, this work needs to be extended to sample more high schools from different regions of the country. Secondly, the samples need to be more racially, ethnically, and socioeconomically heterogeneous and diverse. Finally, it would be extremely valuable to gather interviews with at least some of the students, to explore how they feel about their grades as seniors, and what factors have the most influence on them in these areas.

- It is our fervent hope that we will never get more data to work with, because no new school shootings will ever occur. But there is still much to learn from the data we already have, and other data related to it. It makes sense to use these data to create a more sophisticated model that allows us to predict what sorts of behaviors are particularly likely to lead to violence. Data sources can be expanded to parents, siblings, classmates, teachers, and other people who knew the shooters and who might be able to contribute important insights. Finally, this research can be extended into less dire, but nonetheless serious areas where we need better intervention, especially in the area of bully prevention.

What Have We Accomplished?

Looking back over the entire book so far, we have accomplished a great deal. We have covered the following topics:

- The nature and context of educational research
- A good solid working definition of research literacy
- Qualitative, quantitative, and mixed methods article types
- Qualitative, quantitative, and statistical literacies
- How to read and interpret titles
- How to read and code Abstracts
- How to read and interpret purposes
- How to read and interpret rationales
- How to read and interpret research questions
- How to read and interpret arguments that support research questions
- How to read and interpret references
- How to read and interpret Methods and Procedures sections
- How to read and interpret Quantitative Results and Findings
- How to read and interpret Qualitative Results and Findings
- How to read and interpret Conclusions or Discussions sections

As you can see, this is quite a set of accomplishments. At the same time, however, it is merely the beginning.

In the final chapters, we will look at some more advanced topics that we need to take into account as we get better and better at being research critics. Finally, we will end by looking at the nature of critics in general, and how we can draw wisdom and insight from the critical process in general.

Chapter Twelve

Advanced Concepts
and Techniques

B<small>Y NOW, WE HAVE</small> a very basic and serviceable understanding of how research articles are put together and how to begin reading them in a critical fashion. But there are a series of advanced concepts that we at least need to begin to explore in order to build our critical abilities over time and practice.

Reliability

Before it can be of value in any other way, each and every research study needs to be reliable. In quantitative research, reliability is about how we can make sure that the tools we use to measure concepts and collect data are accurate and stable. There are three major ways to assess reliability in quantitative research.

Test-Based Reliability When tests are used to gather data and measure concepts, there are two ways their stability and accuracy can be evaluated. *Test-retest reliability* is based on using the same test twice, and seeing if you get the same or very similar scores. *Alternate forms reliability* is used when two equivalent forms of the same test are used and the results are compared to each other.

Inter-Rater Reliability Sometimes researchers ask third parties to use rating or code systems to rate or code various observations of responses. Inter-rater reliability is a process where these ratings are compared across raters to see how similar and consistent the ratings are with each other.

Internal Consistency Internal consistency is a process where an item or some subset of items on a test is compared to the test as a whole, to see how well those items or subsets represent the test as a whole. The simplest measure of internal consistency is *split-half reliability*, where a test is divided into even and odd items, and those halves are compared to each other and to the test as a whole. *Inter-item reliability* is a more sophisticated version of this process, where each item in turn is correlated to the test as a whole.

Reliability in Qualitative Research Qualitative data need to be accurate and stable as well. The key concept for qualitative reliability is the notion of trustworthiness. To what degree can the researchers trust the data they are collecting, usually from other people? Trustworthiness can be bolstered by using data that can be confirmed by other participants, and by collecting data from credible sources.

Validity

Another major requirement of each and every research study is that it needs to be valid. In quantitative research, validity is a determination of the degree to which what we claim to measure is actually about what it is that we want to measure, and not something else.

There are five major ways to assess validity in quantitative research.

Face Validity This is actually the weakest way to assess validity, and nearly all the time should not be trusted. Face validity simply means that the measure looks like it should measure what it claims to measure. For instance, a depression test could ask a lot of questions about depression. We need to be careful about face validity because, as we all know, looks can be deceiving.

Content Validity Content validity is a step up from face validity, and can be quite effective if done carefully and set up properly. Content validity is most often established when a new measuring tool is given to experts, and they carefully evaluate its contents and its structure. If the experts are careful and do their job well, the resulting measure can be trusted at least to a degree until stronger measures of validity can be employed.

Criterion Validity This is a stronger mode of validity than many of the others, because it uses empirical testing to make sure its measurements are valid. Criterion validity is used to predict future results or observations, and is upheld when those predictions turn out to be correct. For instance, a test to predict college grades is often validated by comparing student scores on the test to their eventual college grades.

Construct Validity Construct validity deals with those sticky situations where researchers are looking at constructs and not things they can observe or measure directly. For instance, no one can see depression or anxiety or even hunger directly. They are constructs. But we have many ways of measuring things like depression and anxiety and hunger, from clinical observations to reports from experts to scores on well-established tests to even self-report. These well-established modes of looking at constructs can be used to validate newer measures of these constructs.

Validity in Qualitative Research Qualitative data need to be valid as well. The key concept for validity is the notion of triangulation. When triangulation is used, researchers seek to gather data from two or more relevant and credible sources. The more these data converge on each other, the more likely the researchers are looking at what they intended to study.

Error Types

When researchers test hypotheses, they do so using probability tools. That is, researchers can never be 100 percent sure that a given hypothesis is significant or not. Instead, they do so within a probability framework—usually working with either 20 to 1 odds (p<.05) or 100 to 1 odds (p<.01).

In the real world, however, any significance claim is either true or false. That is, if the researchers claim, say, that on the average proper sleep leads to better grades, then that is either true or not. So there is always a distinction between what a test says and what is really the case.

In the best situation, a test result is actually true. That is, when the researchers say that proper rest leads to better grades the data bear them out.

But there are two other possibilities—the test can say a claim is true but it is really false, or the test concludes that the claim is false, but it is really true. These are Type I and Type II errors, respectively. We will look at each in turn:

Type I Error This is often called a *Confidence* error. By this, we mean that we cannot be confident in the researchers' findings. There are two major causes for Type I errors:

- The probability test is too lenient. Instead of using 20 to 1 odds, for instance, the researchers may have used 10 to 1 odds. This is rarely acceptable. Even though 10 to 1 odds look pretty decent, it is not strict enough within the educational research tradition.
- The probability level has not been balanced by the possible risks of making a confidence error. In this case, the researchers may have used a generally acceptable value like 20 to 1 odds, but the circumstances dictate that they needed to be more strict. Here is a real-world example to make this point, not in educational research but in medicine. Suppose a surgeon told you that you had a 20 to 1 chance of surviving an operation. Would you have that operation? It would depend on what the operation was. If it were, say, a face lift, you might be reluctant to risk even a 5 percent chance of mortality on cosmetic surgery. If it were an operation that would save your life, then the odds mean something different and you would most likely do it. Even though the stakes are generally not this high in educational research, failure to consider them can lead to a confidence error.

Type II Error This is often called a *Power* error. By this, we mean that the test of significance was not powerful enough to pick up the fact that the findings were actually significant. There are two major causes for Type II errors:

- The sample size is too small. The smaller the sample size, the more robust the differences have to be in order for the results to be significant. Researchers can try to fix this problem by increasing the sample size.
- The probability level is too high. Suppose the researchers set their probability level at, say, p<.000001. This would mean there would have to be a million to one odds that the results were due to sampling error. There are very few results indeed that could stand up to this stringent a test.

Researchers can try to fix this at the outset by setting a commonly accepted probability level of either 20 to 1 or 100 to 1.

Effect Sizes

When we looked at relationships, hypothesis tests, and models, we placed a great deal of importance on determining whether the findings were statistically significant. But there are times when significance by itself is not enough.

Consider the following example. Suppose we are interested in why middle school students start smoking. We decide to look at the role of, say, video games. Our sample is huge—we gather data on 100,000 middle school students who have started smoking. When we look at the data, we find that there is a significant relationship between hours playing video games and smoking behavior. By significant, we mean that the effect of playing video games is greater than zero. But when we take a closer look, we find out that video games impact only about 3 percent of all middle school kids who smoke. Because our sample is so huge, 3 percent is greater than zero, and so it is significant. But what does it tell us? What kind of payoff would we get if we focused on video games in an anti-smoking program? Unfortunately, not much. Just because an effect is significantly greater than zero does not mean it is worth focusing on. That is why we need to look at effect sizes as well.

There are three key ways to look at effect sizes:

Correlation and Variance The oldest and simplest form of effect size determination involves simple correlation. Consider the following correlation: $r_{(xy)} = +0.80$. As one might expect, if the sample size is even moderately large, this correlation will be significant and therefore there is a direct relationship greater than zero. But with this correlation, you can take it a step further. For precise mathematical reasons, if you square the actual correlation coefficient, you will get the percentage

of common variation between the two variables being correlated. In this case, our correlation of 0.80 actually accounts
for 64 percent of the variation. This is a fairly large effect size,
since there are any number of things that can work together
to account for the remaining 36 percent of the variation.

Hypothesis Testing and Effect Sizes When effect sizes are
computed for t-test and ANOVA data, the various mean differences between (for instance) treatment and control groups
are adjusted by the standard deviation of the two conditions
taken together. The most commonly used tool is the Cohen *d*,
which can be formulated for both t-test and ANOVA studies.
Using the Cohen *d*, effect sizes around 0.20 are in the small
range, effect sizes around 0.50 are in the moderate range, and
effect sizes of 0.80 or greater are large. In this way, a common
metric for evaluating effect sizes can be used.

The Role of Effect Sizes in Meta-Analysis The final situation
where effect sizes are most commonly used is in meta-analyses.
As you may remember, a meta-analysis is a study of studies.
That is, a number of studies that address the same research
area are compared.

There are two goals for these comparisons. First of all, it
is an objective way to determine which studies might be better than others, and so should play a greater role in guiding
future research.

Second of all, since effect sizes take into account a wide
variety of research circumstances, the effect size for each study
can be taken as an index that can be compared directly to
other studies. In this way, researchers can create a distribution of effect sizes, and this distribution can be treated like
any other distribution. So, as a result, the meta-analysis helps
the researchers draw a meta-portrait of a body of research
findings.

Chapter Thirteen

The Research Path

IN THIS FINAL CHAPTER, we would like to take our leave by
showing how becoming research literate and developing our
ongoing skills as research critics are more than just specific
skills. They are part of an ongoing worldview that allows us to
look at our world in new and sophisticated ways.

Taking Stock

We are at the point of this process where we can take stock
of our own development as research critics. How far have we
come? What do we need to do to get better and better?

We can start by looking at the following set of questions
you need to revisit on a regular basis as you seek to hone your
critical skills:

- Am I continuing to practice my critical craft on a regular
  basis?
- Am I staying current in the knowledge-base of educational
  research in general?
- Am I staying current in the knowledge-base of educational
  research literacy and criticism in particular?

- Are there areas of weakness in my technical knowledge that I need to add or refine?
- Do I seek feedback and guidance from my fellow research critics in order to hone my skills?
- Am I using my skills and efforts in the best possible way to improve the field of educational research as a whole?

So long as you keep your eye on these and related issues, you will not go astray.

The Community of Critics

We can also benefit by thinking about how the educational research critic is part of the larger fellowship of critics. This not only keeps us from feeling isolated in our rather narrow and specialized framework, but it helps us feel connected with the best aspects of the critical perspective, regardless of the field.

Therefore, we need to look toward the larger community of critics. What do all critics share in common, and what do all critics need to do to get better and better at their craft?

Here are some of the most important common threads all critics and critical activities have in common:

- Critics need to know what they are doing. Movie critics do not have to make movies and art critics do not have to make art, but they have to know what movies and art are, and how to tell the differences between good movies and good art, and bad movies and bad art. The same is true for critics of educational research. We have to know enough about both education and research to make proper judgments of worth and value.
- Critics have to be proficient in their grasp of technical skills. If you are evaluating qualitative research, you need to know and understand the tenets of qualitative research. If you are looking at multivariate research, you need to know how that type of research operates at both the conceptual

and technical levels. Technical aspects of educational research change and expand and evolve every day, and you need to be as up-to-date with these trends as you possibly can be. At the same time, you also need to remember what technical knowledge and skills form the backbone of understanding educational research, and keep a firm grasp and perspective of these skills.

- Critics need to be proficient in terms of their critical skills. There are rules and guidelines for everything, including being a critic. You need to know how those rules apply to educational research, and follow them diligently. As our critical understanding improves and expands, you need to also improve and expand your own skills.

- Critics have to be honest, fair, and trustworthy. People turn to them for guidance, and that guidance has to be based on the work itself, not on any whims or grudges or quirks of the critic. Constructive criticism can ultimately be unintentionally devastating without being destructive criticism. Destructive criticism harms everyone, including the critic.

The Road Ahead

Finally, we will take our leave by looking at the path of research as it stretches out before us. There are three basic ideas we want to address in parting.

Research as a Starting Point

It is very important to get into the habit of looking at every problem, every glitch, or every unclear or confusing situation as a valid starting point for research. If this is a problem for you, chances are that it has been a problem that others have looked at as well. So don't hesitate to go look for the research. In this age of the Internet and comprehensive databases, the odds are with you. We recommend developing your own style of searching for information, and then working with others to see how you can collectively refine and improve your search for important and relevant research.

Research as a Destination

The next key point is to realize that there are no starting and ending points in research. There is no such thing as the individual researcher working off alone by himself or herself. Research is an inherently social process. When researchers start their work, they build on the work of others. When their careers are over, they leave their paths for others to follow and pursue. A good metaphor for the research process is the relay race. Researchers do not start the race or end the race. They are like the middle runners, taking the baton from others and passing it along for others when they are done.

Research as Play

Finally, we leave you with something we have discovered by looking at the many fine researchers we have known over the years. In each and every case, every single great researcher has looked at research as a form of play. They attack the research process with great gusto and vigor, and it shows in their work. Do not be afraid to critique research in terms of its liveliness, or lack thereof. It is not enough to allow research to be merely competent. We need great research, and great research requires great researchers playing their hearts out!

And so we come to the end of this particular work about the role of research, research literacy, and the research critic in education. All of us are beginners in this process, but we hope that we have shown you a few pointers to allow your journey along this path to be a bit easier, a bit more useful, and hopefully more rewarding.

Just remember to keep your eye on the path.

Appendix A

Guidelines for Article Evaluation

Here is a series of questions to ask as you approach any article in educational research:

- Is this a *quantitative, qualitative,* or *mixed methods* article? How can you tell?
- If the article is *quantitative,* which of the following *designs* does it employ—organizing data, discovering relationships, testing hypotheses, building explanatory and/or predictive models?
- If the article is *qualitative,* which of the following *designs* does it employ—discovering meaning, investigating meaning, illuminating understanding, making things better?
- What sort of *title* does it have—*equation, process, situation, theoretical,* or *indirect*? What does the *title* tell you about the article from the very start?
- Is there an Abstract? If so, how would you decode it? What can the Abstract tell you about the article in general?
- What is the *purpose* of the article—exploration, extension, expansion, correction?

- What is the *rationale* of the article—crisis, importance, depth, gap-filling, commitment?
- How many *research questions* are there? Are they explicitly labeled, or did you have to dig them out?
- What sort of *argument* is used—setup, support, or setup and support? Is the argument clear and well-stated?
- How many *references* are there? What is the time span, from oldest to newest? How many references are less than five years old, given the publication date of the article? How many references from the same researchers or team of researchers are cited? How many basic topics are covered?
- What sorts of *sampling* strategies are used?
- What kinds of *data gathering* methods and special *instrumentation* techniques are used, if any?
- How is the design of the study operationalized?
- How are the various *analysis techniques* needed to answer the research questions of the study operationalized?
- Are there any special *time* issues, such as a longitudinal design or pre-post measures, involved?
- Is there anything about *location* or *place* issues that is unique enough to make the article special?
- If the article is *quantitative*, which of the following types of *findings* are reported—descriptive statistics, measures and patterns of frequencies, measures and patterns of relationships, tests of hypotheses, significant aspects of predictive/ explanatory models?
- What statistical tools are used for each of the processes above? How did these analyses address the research questions of the article?
- If the article is *qualitative*, which of the following types of *findings* are reported—demographic data, basic observations, confirmed vs. unconfirmed assumptions, new insights, new understandings, improved situations?
- How were the data discussed above used to sort and organize the findings, reflect and synthesize insights and discoveries, take stock of expected and unexpected phenomena,

and tell what happened in the study in an overall and global narrative?

- Which of the following topics are covered in the Discussions or Conclusions section—summary, explanation, implications, expansion?
- Which of the following *advanced quantitative concepts*, if any, are addressed—reliability, validity, error types, effect sizes?
- If the article is *qualitative*, which of the following "sins," if any, does it fall prey to—appropriation, competitiveness, narcissism, rigidity, sentimentality, superficiality, timidity?
- How has engaging with the article furthered your development as a research critic? What insights from other critics, both inside and outside the field of education and educational research, can you bring to bear to improve your ability to engage in articles like this in the future?

Appendix B

Dissecting an Article

THE FOLLOWING IS A very short example of an imaginary article we wrote to show how all the features of the guidelines can come into play.

Using Play Foods to Teach Nutrition to Preschoolers in Head Start Programs

(This is a process—the process in question is teaching nutrition. Note how the researchers use the title to focus clearly on the intent of the research.)

Abstract

(Here is the Abstract.)

The purpose of this study is to see if selected play foods can be used to teach basic nutrition to preschool children. Thirty preschool children were randomly selected from an urban Head Start cohort of Title I families. As part of a pre-post design, the children were first given a sorting task based on nutrition and then given food models to play with. On a repeat sorting task, their ability to sort foods into proper nutrition groups was improved significantly, as determined by a repeated measures t-test. Given that preschool children from poor settings often do not get proper nutritional guidance, these results were encouraging.

(*Here is the coded Abstract.*)

[PURPOSE] The purpose of this study is to see if [PROBLEM] selected play foods can be used to teach basic nutrition to preschool children. [PARTICIPANTS] Thirty preschool children were randomly selected from an urban Head Start cohort of Title I families. [DESIGN] As part of a pre-post design, the children were first given a sorting task based on nutrition and then given food models to play with. On a repeat sorting task, [RESULTS] their ability to sort foods into proper nutrition groups was improved significantly, [ANALYSIS] as determined by a repeated measures t-test. [CONCLUSIONS] Given that preschool children from poor settings often do not get proper nutritional guidance, these results were encouraging.

Introduction

(*This is the beginning part of the article and should contain the* purpose, rationale, research question, *and the* argument.)

(*This is an* importance *rationale, because it focuses on the importance of early nutritional education.*)
Poor children often have limited access to proper nutritional information (Delta, 2011). Because of this, they may manifest

poor nutritional understanding and decision-making for the rest of their lives. Therefore, the earlier nutritional education can start, the more potentially useful it will be (Alpha, Foxtrot & Zulu, 2009).

(*This is part of the* argument, *which is either a* setup *or* setup and support *argument, depending on the location of the* research question.)

Teaching nutrition, which is a complex topic, to very young children poses a challenge to the educational community (Delta, 2011). Young children often do not possess the sorts of complex cognitive processes necessary to understand the links between food and health.

Recent research, however, suggests that play can be used as a way to teach more complex concepts to young children (Bravo, 1998). Concepts in areas such as safety (Victor & Golf, 2003; Yankee & Victor, 2007; Yankee, Golf & Victor, 2011), hygiene (Alpha & Foxtrot, 2008; Zulu & Alpha, 2012), and listening comprehension (Whiskey, Echo & Charlie, 2007; Charlie & Whiskey, 2009; Hotel, Echo & Whiskey, 2011; Whiskey, Echo, Hotel & Charlie, 2013) have been successfully advanced using play.

(*This is the* purpose *of the article, which is an* extension *purpose.*)

The purpose of this study is to see if these play methods can be extended into the realm of teaching young children about nutrition.

(*This is the* research question, *which is based on a* setup *argument, because it comes at the end of the Introduction.*)

The following research question was raised: Can selected play foods be used to teach young poor children the basics of good nutrition?

Methods

(This is the part of the article where the methods used to answer the research question are described.)

(This is the sample.*)*
In this study, 30 preschool children were randomly selected from a pool of 285 children in an urban Head Start program. All children were between the ages of 3 and 5, and they all came from homes covered by Title I programs. Median income for families in this Head Start program is below the federal poverty level.

(This is the instrumentation.*)*
The following three nutritional concepts were identified: Build Strong Muscles, Build Strong Bones, and Keep You Going. Each of these nutritional concepts was operationalized by wooden tiles containing the picture of a common food. There were three common foods for each group, as follows:

* Build Strong Muscles—Hamburger, Chicken Leg, Egg
* Build Strong Bones—Milk Carton, Cheese, Yogurt
* Keep You Going—Bread, Cereal, Plate of Pasta

(This is the pre- *section of the* pre-post design.*)*
Before the play session, each child is asked to sort the nine foods into one of the three categories.

(This is the basic design *of the study.*)*
After this sorting was completed and recorded for each child, the children then participated in a playgroup. Actual models of all nine foods were used, and children were encouraged to form small groups and play with these models. Researchers circulated among the groups of children and guided them in choosing foods for particular uses to help them grow up strong and healthy.

(*The second sorting task was the* post *part of the* pre-post design.)

The children were then given a snack of juice and carrot sticks and asked to perform the sorting task again.

(*The snack was offered to control for possible hunger effects, using foods that were neutral to the study.*)

Results

(*Here is where the actual findings are presented.*)

(*These are the* descriptive *statistics for the data.*)
The following data were reported:

    Pre-Sorting Correct Assignment: mean = 2.67
    standard deviation = 0.98
    Post-Sorting Correct Assignment: mean = 5.83
    standard deviation = 1.42

(*This is the* test *of the* hypothesis *that the play increased the sorting ability, which reflects an improved cognitive understanding.*)

A repeated measures t-test was then conducted on these data, and the results were as follows:

$$t(df = 29) = 13.78* \quad *p<.05$$

As indicated by the t-test, the correct matching scores were significantly higher after the free play with the food forms.

Discussion

(*Here is where the* results *are discussed and* conclusions *are drawn regarding the data.*)

(*This is the* summary *of the* results.)
The results support our claim that play can improve cognitive understanding of nutritional concepts for children from very poor backgrounds.

(*These are the* implications *of the study.*)
This is an encouraging finding for several reasons. First of all, it shows that nutritional concepts can be addressed at a very young age. Secondly, it shows that young children from poor backgrounds can learn these basic nutritional concepts. This is extremely important, since poor people often exhibit little understanding of good nutritional concepts, given the many poor food choices they make for themselves and their children (Delta, 2011).

(*These are the* explanations *of the study.*)
There are several concerns with the study, however. First of all, the actual choices offered the children were quite limited. Is it possible to include more choices, and more categories, given their relative lack of cognitive sophistication at their young ages? Furthermore, we used a free play model. Would it be better to use a more standardized model of play, to see if we can test the development of their understandings more precisely?

(*This is the* expansion *of the study.*)
We would like to conclude with a few suggestions for further research. It would be useful to see if expanding both the food list and the concept list is feasible for young children. It would also be interesting to see how young children from poor backgrounds compare to middle-class children of the same age. Finally, it would be interesting to expand the research to look at older children, at various levels, to see how we might teach these nutritional concepts to them.

References

(These are the articles cited in the study. They are first presented in standard alphabetical order.)

Alpha, A. & Foxtrot, F. (2008). Teaching hygiene concepts to preschool children using play. *Journal of Childhood Hygiene, 23,* 211–234.

Alpha, A., Foxtrot, F. & Zulu, Z. (2009). Using the wooden block method to teach hygiene to children. *Hygiene, 45,* 9–37.

Bravo, B. (1998). *How children play.* New York: Kelty Press.

Charlie, C. & Whiskey, W. (2009). Testing listening comprehension in noisy play settings. *Childhood Comprehension Reports, 2,* 87–96.

Delta, D. (2011). *Basics of pediatric nutrition.* London: Royal Thames Culbertson.

Hotel, H., Echo, E. & Whiskey, W. (2011). Testing listening comprehension in multicultural play settings. *Childhood Comprehension Reports, 4,* 113–165.

Victor, V. & Golf, G. (2003). Teaching safety concepts to preschool children using play. *Journal of Childhood Safety, 23,* 211–234.

Whiskey, W., Echo, E. & Charlie, C. (2007). Teaching listening comprehension to preschool children using play. *Journal of Childhood Comprehension, 23,* 211–234.

Whiskey, W., Echo, E., Hotel, H. & Charlie, C. (2013). *Preschool listening comprehension and preschool play.* Boston: Preschool Primer Research Press.

Yankee, Y., Golf, G. & Victor, V. (2011). Safety learning in afterschool settings. *Journal of Afterschool Learning, 21,* 67–122.

Yankee, Y. & Victor, V. (2007). Identifying basic safety concepts for young children using play self-reports. *Journal of Pediatric Self-Report, 33,* 23–45.

Zulu, Z. & Alpha, A. (2012). Expanding hygiene education by play from preschool to kindergarten. *Journal of Basic Kindergarten Research, 65,* 1066–1078.

(Now they are presented in chronological order.)

Bravo, B. (1998). *How children play.* New York: Kelty Press.

Victor, V. & Golf, G. (2003). Teaching safety concepts to preschool children using play. *Journal of Childhood Safety, 23,* 211–234.

Whiskey, W., Echo, E. & Charlie, C. (2007). Teaching listening comprehension to preschool children using play. *Journal of Childhood Comprehension*, 23, 211–234.

Yankee, Y. & Victor, V. (2007). Identifying basic safety concepts for young children using play self-reports. *Journal of Pediatric Self-Report*, 33, 23–45.

Alpha, A. & Foxtrot, F. (2008). Teaching hygiene concepts to preschool children using play. *Journal of Childhood Hygiene*, 23, 211–234.

Alpha, A., Foxtrot, F. & Zulu, Z. (2009). Using the wooden block method to teach hygiene to children. *Hygiene*, 45, 9–37.

Charlie, C. & Whiskey, W. (2009). Testing listening comprehension in noisy play settings. *Childhood Comprehension Reports*, 2, 87–96.

Delta, D. (2011). *Basics of pediatric nutrition*. London: Royal Thames Culbertson.

Hotel, H., Echo, E. & Whiskey, W. (2011). Testing listening comprehension in multicultural play settings. *Childhood Comprehension Reports*, 4, 113–165.

Yankee, Y., Golf, G. & Victor, V. (2011). Safety learning in afterschool settings. *Journal of Afterschool Learning*, 21, 67–122.

Zulu, Z. & Alpha, A. (2012). Expanding hygiene education by play from preschool to kindergarten. *Journal of Basic Kindergarten Research*, 65, 1066–1078.

Whiskey, W., Echo, E., Hotel, H. & Charlie, C. (2013). *Preschool listening comprehension and preschool play*. Boston: Preschool Primer Research Press.

(*Now they are presented by teams.*)

(*This is the Alpha team.*)
Alpha, A. & Foxtrot, F. (2008). Teaching hygiene concepts to preschool children using play. *Journal of Childhood Hygiene*, 23, 211–234.

Alpha, A., Foxtrot, F. & Zulu, Z. (2009). Using the wooden block method to teach hygiene to children. *Hygiene*, 45, 9–37.

Zulu, Z. & Alpha, A. (2012). Expanding hygiene education by play from preschool to kindergarten. *Journal of Basic Kindergarten Research*, 65, 1066–1078.

(*This is the Victor team.*)

Victor, V. & Golf, G. (2003). Teaching safety concepts to preschool children using play. *Journal of Childhood Safety*, 23, 211–234.

Yankee, Y. & Victor, V. (2007). Identifying basic safety concepts for young children using play self-reports. *Journal of Pediatric Self-Report*, 33, 23–45.

Yankee, Y., Golf, G. & Victor, V. (2011). Safety learning in afterschool settings. *Journal of Afterschool Learning*, 21, 67–122.

(*This is the Whiskey team.*)

Whiskey, W., Echo, E. & Charlie, C. (2007). Teaching listening comprehension to preschool children using play. *Journal of Childhood Comprehension*, 23, 211–234.

Charlie, C. & Whiskey, W. (2009). Testing listening comprehension in noisy play settings. *Childhood Comprehension Reports*, 2, 87–96.

Hotel, H., Echo, E. & Whiskey, W. (2011). Testing listening comprehension in multicultural play settings. *Childhood Comprehension Reports*, 4, 113–165.

Whiskey, W., Echo, E., Hotel, H. & Charlie, C. (2013). *Preschool listening comprehension and preschool play*. Boston: Preschool Primer Research Press.

(*Now they are presented by topic.*)

(*This is the Safety and Play topic.*)

Victor, V. & Golf, G. (2003). Teaching safety concepts to preschool children using play. *Journal of Childhood Safety*, 23, 211–234.

Yankee, Y. & Victor, V. (2007). Identifying basic safety concepts for young children using play self-reports. *Journal of Pediatric Self-Report*, 33, 23–45.

Yankee, Y., Golf, G. & Victor, V. (2011). Safety learning in afterschool settings. *Journal of Afterschool Learning*, 21, 67–122.

Bravo, B. (1998). *How children play*. New York: Kelty Press.

(*This is the Hygiene and Nutrition topic.*)

Alpha, A. & Foxtrot, F. (2008). Teaching hygiene concepts to preschool children using play. *Journal of Childhood Hygiene*, 23, 211–234.

Alpha, A., Foxtrot, F. & Zulu, Z. (2009). Using the wooden block method to teach hygiene to children. *Hygiene*, 45, 9–37.

Zulu, Z. & Alpha, A. (2012). Expanding hygiene education by play from preschool to kindergarten. *Journal of Basic Kindergarten Research*, 65, 1066–1078.

Delta, D. (2011). *Basics of pediatric nutrition*. London: Royal Thames Culbertson.

(*This is the Listening Comprehension topic.*)

Whiskey, W., Echo, E. & Charlie, C. (2007). Teaching listening comprehension to preschool children using play. *Journal of Childhood Comprehension*, 23, 211–234.

Charlie, C. & Whiskey, W. (2009). Testing listening comprehension in noisy play settings. *Childhood Comprehension Reports*, 2, 87–96.

Hotel, H., Echo, E. & Whiskey, W. (2011). Testing listening comprehension in multicultural play settings. *Childhood Comprehension Reports*, 4, 113–165.

Whiskey, W., Echo, E., Hotel, H. & Charlie, C. (2013). *Preschool listening comprehension and preschool play*. Boston: Preschool Primer Research Press.

References

Adler, M. J. & Van Doren, C. (1972). *How to read a book: The classic guide to intelligent reading.* New York: Simon & Schuster.

Bloom, H. (2001). *How to read and why.* New York: Simon & Schuster.

Bogdan, R. C. & Biklen, S. K. (2007). *Qualitative research for education: An introduction to theory and methods* (5E). Boston, MA: Allyn and Bacon.

Booth, W. C., Colomb, G. G. & Williams, J. M. (2008). *The craft of research* (3E). Chicago, IL: University of Chicago Press.

Campbell, D. T. & Stanley, J. C. (1966). *Experimental and quasi-experimental designs for research.* Boston, MA: Houghton Mifflin.

Chambers, J. M., Cleveland, W. S., Kleiner, B. & Tukey, P. A. (1983). *Graphical methods for data analysis.* Belmont, CA: Wadsworth.

Clark, C. (2001). BIO 190—Writing an abstract. California State Polytechnic University, Pomona. Retrieved from http://www.csupomona.edu/~jcclark/classes/bio190/abstract.html.

Cresswell, J. W. (2011). *Educational research: Planning, conducting, and evaluating quantitative and qualitative research* (4E). Upper Saddle River, NJ: Prentice Hall.

Crotty, M. (1998). *The foundations of social research: Meaning and perspective in the research process.* Thousand Oaks, CA: Sage.

December, J. & Katz, S. (2003). Abstracts. Rensselaer Polytechnic Institute. Retrieved from http://www.rpi.edu/dept/llc/writecenter/web/abstracts.html.

Denzin, N. K. & Lincoln, Y. S. (2011). *The SAGE handbook of qualitative research.* Thousand Oaks, CA: Sage.

Evans, J. D. (1996). *Straightforward statistics for the behavioral sciences.* Pacific Grove, CA: Brooks/Cole.

Fielding, N. G., Lee, R. M. & Blank, G. (2008). *The SAGE handbook of online research methods.* London: Sage.

Folks, J. L. (1981). *Ideas of statistics.* New York: Wiley.

Glaser, B. G. & Strauss, A. L. (1967). *The discovery of grounded theory: Strategies for qualitative research.* Chicago: Aldine Publishing Company.

Hittleman, D. R. & Simon, A. J. (2005). *Interpreting educational research: An introduction for consumers of research* (4E). Upper Saddle River, NJ: Prentice Hall.

Hopkins, D. (2002). *A teacher's guide to classroom research* (3E). Buckingham: Open University Press.

Hubbard, R. S. & Power, B. M. (2003). *The art of classroom inquiry: A handbook for teacher researchers* (2E). Portsmouth, NH: Heinemann.

Huck, S. W. (2011). *Reading statistics and research* (6E). New York: Longman.

Keeley, S. (2003). *The Prentice Hall guide to evaluating online resources.* Upper Saddle River, NJ: Prentice Hall.

Kies, D. (2003). Writing an abstract. College of Dupage. Retrieved from http://papyr.com/hypertextbooks/engl_102/abstract .htm.

Kincheloe, J. L. (2002). *Teachers as researchers: Qualitative inquiry as a path to empowerment* (2E). New York: Routledge Falmer.

Kranzler, J. H. (2010). *Statistics for the terrified* (5E). Upper Saddle River, NJ: Prentice Hall.

Krathwohl, D. R. (2004). *Methods of educational and social science research: An integrated approach* (2E). New York: Longman.

Lancy, D. F. (1993). *Qualitative research in education: An introduction to the major traditions.* New York: Longman.

Lincoln, Y. S. & Guba, E. G. (1982). *Naturalistic inquiry.* Newbury Park, CA: Sage.

McLaren, P. (2006). *Life in schools* (5E). New York: Longman.

McMillan, J. H. (2011). *Educational research: Fundamentals for the consumer* (6E). New York: Addison Wesley Longman.

Merriam, S. B. (1998). *Qualitative research and case study applications in education.* San Francisco, CA: Jossey-Bass.

Miles, M. B. & Huberman, A. M. (1994). *Qualitative data analysis* (2E). Thousand Oaks, CA: Sage.

Minium, E. W., Clarke, R. C. & Coladarci, T. (1999). *Elements of statistical reasoning* (2E). New York: Wiley.

Morgan, D. L. (1998). *The focus group guidebook.* Thousand Oaks, CA: Sage.

Moustakas, C. (1994). *Phenomenological research methods.* Thousand Oaks, CA: Sage.

Ong, W. J. (1982). *Orality and literacy: The technologizing of the word.* London: Routledge.

Patton, M. Q. (2001). *Qualitative evaluation and research methods* (3E). Newbury Park, CA: Sage.

Phillips, J. L. (2000). *How to think about statistics* (6E). New York: Freeman.

Salsburg, D. (2002). *The lady tasting tea: How statistics revolutionized science in the twentieth century.* New York: Freeman.

Schreiber, J. B, Stage, F. K., King, J., Nora, A. & Barlow, E. A. (2006). Reporting structural equation modeling and confirmatory factor analysis results: A review. *Journal of Educational Research,* 99, 323–337.

Shank, G. D. (2005). *Qualitative research: A personal skills approach* (2E). Upper Saddle River, NJ: Prentice Hall.

Siegel, S. & Castellan, N. J., Jr. (1988). *Nonparametric statistics for the behavioral sciences* (2E). New York: McGraw-Hill.

Spradley, J. P. (1980). *Participant observation.* New York: Holt, Rinehart & Winston.

Stake, R. E. (1995). *The art of case study research.* Thousand Oaks, CA: Sage.

Strauss, A. & Corbin, J. (2007). *Basics of qualitative research: Techniques and procedures for developing grounded theory* (3E). Thousand Oaks, CA: Sage.

Stringer, E. (2004). *Action research in education.* Upper Saddle River, NJ: Prentice Hall.

Strunk, W., Jr. & White, E. B. (1979). *The elements of style* (3E). New York: Macmillan.

van Belle, G. (2008). *Statistical rules of thumb* (2E). New York: Wiley.

Wainer, H. (1992). Understanding graphs and tables. *Educational Researcher,* 21(1), 14–23.

Weinberg, G. H. & Schumaker, J. A (1997). *Statistics: An intuitive approach* (4E). Belmont, CA: Wadsworth.

Williams, F. & Monge, P. (2001). *Reasoning with statistics: How to read quantitative research* (5E). Fort Worth, TX: Harcourt.

Wink, J. (2010). *Critical pedagogy: Notes from the real world* (4E). New York: Addison Wesley Longman.

Wolcott, H. F. (2004). *The art of fieldwork* (2E). Walnut Creek, CA: Altamira Press.

Index

About the Authors

Gary Shank, Professor of Education at Duquesne University, is the author of *Qualitative Research: A Personal Skills Approach*.

Launcelot Brown is Associate Professor of Educational Research and Chair of the Department of Educational Foundations and Leadership at Duquesne University. He served as an Associate Editor for the *Journal of Educational Measurement* from 2006 to 2009.

Janice Pringle is Associate Professor of Pharmacy and Therapeutics at the University of Pittsburgh.

Made in the USA
Middletown, DE
08 January 2018